Air Combat

Afterburners lit, an F-15E Strike Eagle can accelerate at a pace that would take an automobile from zero to sixty miles per hour in one second. Adapted from the world's premier air-superiority fighter, the E model has lost nothing of earlier versions' dogfighting prowess.

A battle-ready F-15 carries eight air-to-air missiles. Hung under the wings are a quartet of heat-seeking Sidewinders for short-range shots; nestled against the fuselage are four radar-guided Sparrows for use at ranges of up to sixty miles or so.

An F-16 breaks left in a vain attempt
to elude an F/A-18 Hornet in hot combat, as the two planes struggle in mock combat at Top Gun, the U.S. Navy's graduate
school for fighter pilots.

A Sparrow missile leaps from the rail of an F-14 Tomcat. Launched from behind a target at a range of about five miles, and closing at twice the speed of sound, a Sparrow can give its victim less than ten seconds to attempt an escape.

Wings fanned out and flaps lowered for maximum lift, an F-14 slams down on the deck of the supercarrier *Nimitz* at 150 miles per hour. One of four arrester cables lying across the deck will haul the twenty-ton fighter to a stop.

Other Publications:

TIME-LIFE LIBRARY OF CURIOUS AND UNUSUAL FACTS
AMERICAN COUNTRY
VOYAGE THROUGH THE UNIVERSE
THE THIRD REICH
THE TIME-LIFE GARDENER'S GUIDE
MYSTERIES OF THE UNKNOWN
TIME FRAME
FIX IT YOURSELF
FITNESS, HEALTH & NUTRITION
SUCCESSFUL PARENTING
HEALTHY HOME COOKING
UNDERSTANDING COMPUTERS
LIBRARY OF NATIONS
THE ENCHANTED WORLD
THE KODAK LIBRARY OF CREATIVE PHOTOGRAPHY
GREAT MEALS IN MINUTES
THE CIVIL WAR
PLANET EARTH
COLLECTOR'S LIBRARY OF THE CIVIL WAR
THE EPIC OF FLIGHT
THE GOOD COOK
WORLD WAR II
HOME REPAIR AND IMPROVEMENT
THE OLD WEST

For information on and a full description of any
of the Time-Life Books series listed above,
please call 1-800-621-7026 or write:
Reader Information
Time-Life Customer Service
P.O. Box C-32068
Richmond, Virginia 23261-2068

THE NEW FACE OF WAR

Air Combat

BY THE EDITORS OF
TIME-LIFE BOOKS, ALEXANDRIA, VIRGINIA

CONSULTANTS

PAUL BACON is the manager of F/A-18 Training Systems Marketing at Hughes Aircraft Company, Manhattan Beach, California. He is a former U.S. Marine Corps experimental test pilot and the first Marine pilot to fly the F/A-18.

LIEUTENANT COLONEL NELSON L. BEARD is a U.S. Air Force fighter pilot with over 2,000 hours' flying time in F-4 Phantoms. In 1983 he was awarded Egyptian Air Force wings while flying F-4s in Cairo. He has also flown extensively in Europe and the Pacific as well as the Middle East.

LIEUTENANT COLONEL CHARLES L. BUZZE has logged over 3,000 hours as a fighter pilot. Now retired from the U.S. Air Force, he held several command positions in the F-15 Division of the Fighter Weapons School, Nellis Air Force Base, Nevada. He is currently director of Air Force Programs, Northrop Corporation.

CAPTAIN BOBBY D'ANGELO, a pilot in the U.S. Air Force Reserve, serves with the 482nd Tactical Fighter Wing. He has trained with Air Combat Maneuvering Instrumentation for the past ten years and was involved with its installation at Homestead Air Force Base, Florida.

LIEUTENANT COLONEL KARL J. ESCHMANN is the director of advanced projects for the Advanced Medium-Range Air-to-Air Missile Program at Eglin Air Force Base, Florida.

LIEUTENANT COLONEL JOHN F. GUILMARTIN, retired from the U.S. Air Force, is associate professor of history at Ohio State University and lectures extensively on the Vietnam War. He flew 120 combat helicopter search-and-rescue missions, mostly over Laos and North Vietnam.

RICHARD P. HALLION is the Charles A. Lindbergh Professor of Aerospace History at the National Air and Space Museum, Smithsonian Institution, Washington, D.C. He has written numerous works on the history of aerospace technology and military aviation.

STEVE KNIGHT is a field engineer with Cubic Defense Systems at Homestead Air Force Base. He has been involved with both design and maintenance of Tactical Aircrew Combat Training System/Air-Combat Maneuvering Instrumentation systems around the world for the past thirteen years.

DAVID A. KRAMER is a vice president of the Radar Systems Group of Hughes Aircraft Company and manager of the group's Advanced Programs Division in El Segundo, California; he was lead designer of the radar system of the F-15.

MAJOR LINCOLN QUIGLEY is an F-4 Phantom II fighter pilot who has participated in ten Red Flag exercises. He has flown with or against the naval and air arms of twelve nations, accumulating over 3,100 hours in various models of the Phantom.

ROBERT L. SHAW, president of Fighter Command, International, is the author of *Fighter Combat: Tactics and Maneuvering*. Once a commander in the U.S. Navy Reserve, he now holds the rank of lieutenant colonel in the U.S. Air Force Reserve.

COLONEL T. C. SKANCHY, recently retired from the U.S. Air Force, commanded the F-15 Division, Fighter Weapons School, and was the vice commander of Red Flag, both at Nellis Air Force Base, Nevada.

CONTENTS

The New Age of the Dogfight

Bursting through the sound barrier during a training exercise in the South China Sea, an F-14A Tomcat trails a cone of vapor spawned by a shock wave. Such a visible signature of supersonic flight is rare, occurring only in conditions of high humidity.

On the morning of January 4, 1989, two F-14 Tomcats from the aircraft carrier *John F. Kennedy*'s Squadron VF-32—call sign Gypsy—were on routine patrol 20,000 feet over the Mediterranean, seventy miles north of Tobruk on the Libyan coast. So far out at sea, the risk of confrontation with Libyan forces seemed remote, but the prospect could not be ruled out completely. Three times in the past eight years the two countries had exchanged military blows.

In 1981, U.S. carrier jets had downed two Libyan planes after being fired upon. In March 1986, the Navy had deliberately challenged Libyan dictator Muammar al-Qadhafi's so-called line of death across the Gulf of Sidra, which he had claimed as a Libyan lake. When Qadhafi sent out gunboats in response, the Navy promptly sank two and destroyed a radar installation ashore. The following month President Ronald Reagan, citing evidence derived from communications intercepts that Libya had sponsored a bomb attack on U.S. servicemen in Berlin, sent fighter-bombers to attack terrorist training facilities and other targets in and around the Libyan capital of Tripoli, almost killing Qadhafi himself.

Now there was another bone of contention between these two antagonists. The United States charged Libya with using a huge chemical plant southwest of Tripoli to produce poison gas and nerve agents. American leaders refused to rule out the possibility of a preemptive strike against the facility.

In this tense atmosphere, Qadhafi had stepped up air activity in the vicinity of the U.S. Sixth Fleet, which was operating in the Mediterranean. This is a standard drill conducted in all the world's oceans, as adversaries shadow each other's vessels or play fighter tag. Before January 4, whenever Libyan planes approached the *Kennedy* or any other U.S. ship, F-14s on combat air patrol (CAP) intercepted the intruders and escorted them away without incident.

17

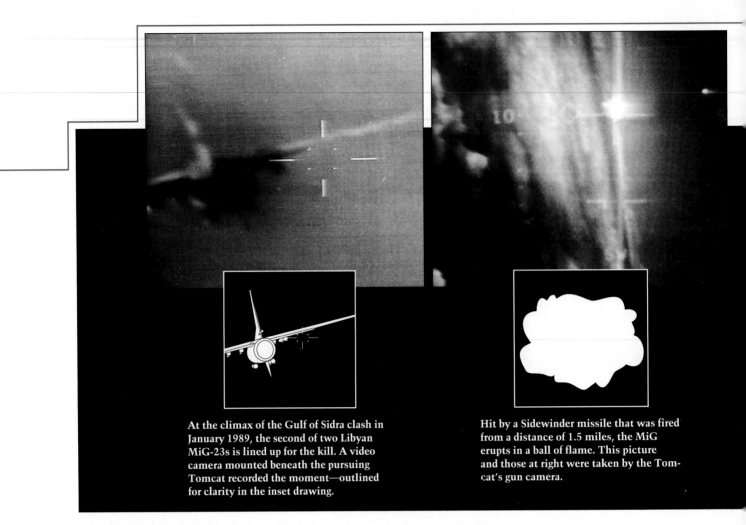

At the climax of the Gulf of Sidra clash in January 1989, the second of two Libyan MiG-23s is lined up for the kill. A video camera mounted beneath the pursuing Tomcat recorded the moment—outlined for clarity in the inset drawing.

Hit by a Sidewinder missile that was fired from a distance of 1.5 miles, the MiG erupts in a ball of flame. This picture and those at right were taken by the Tomcat's gun camera.

The maneuvers had become routine. Nearing a flight of Libyan fighters, the Tomcats would turn to the right or left, then circle in the opposite direction to close on the bogeys from behind. Approaching aircraft bent on attack would not passively accept this maneuver, which placed a flight of Tomcats in an optimum position to knock them down. For that purpose, each of the F-14s carried four Sparrow medium-range radar-guided missiles, four Sidewinder short-range heat seekers, and a 20-mm Vulcan cannon.

Three of the four crewmen on Gypsy flight this day were graduates of Top Gun, the Navy's tactics school for the best of its fighter crews. That men of such caliber had been assigned to patrol duty that morning may have been coincidence, but it is also possible that U.S. intelligence gatherers had intercepted Libyan communications that carried a forecast of hostile intent. In a morning briefing, VF-32's commanding officer had described the upcoming flight as a "good deal" mission—a chance for one or both crews to win laurels.

Five minutes before noon, an E-2C Hawkeye surveillance aircraft, launched from the *Kennedy* and flying a circular course north of the F-14s, sounded an alert. Seconds earlier, the air intercept controller aboard the Hawkeye, probing deep into Libyan air space with radar much more powerful than those aboard the Tomcats,

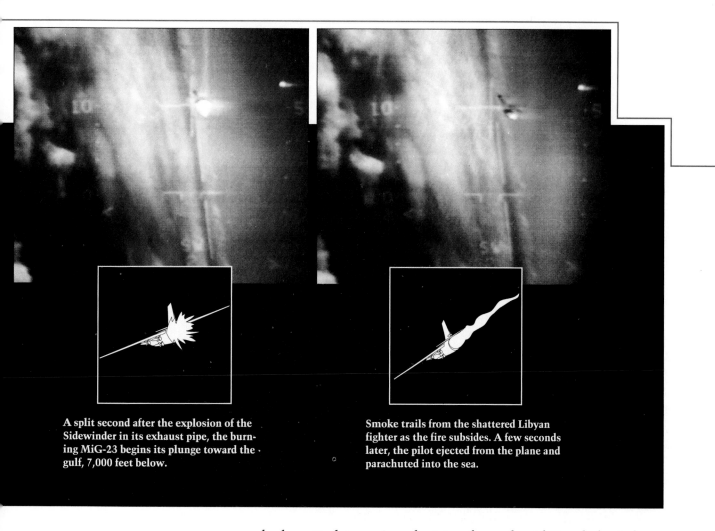

A split second after the explosion of the Sidewinder in its exhaust pipe, the burning MiG-23 begins its plunge toward the gulf, 7,000 feet below.

Smoke trails from the shattered Libyan fighter as the fire subsides. A few seconds later, the pilot ejected from the plane and parachuted into the sea.

had spotted two aircraft rising from the Al-Bumbah air base near Tobruk and heading toward the *Kennedy.*

Ordered by the air warfare commander aboard their ship to intercept the planes, Gypsy flight turned toward the Libyan aircraft and accelerated to 500 knots. As the range diminished, both radar intercept officers (RIOs) monitored the bogeys on their radarscopes using a mode called track-while-scan, in which the radar provides the RIO with detailed information about all of the blips on the screen. Then the Tomcats began the maneuver that would let them intercept from behind. But the Libyan MiGs, instead of holding their course, turned toward the F-14s, seemingly guided by a ground controller whose radio transmissions the Hawkeye's crew could overhear. The Libyans and Americans were less than fifty-three nautical miles apart and closing rapidly when the Tomcats tried again to circle the approaching jets, this time in the opposite direction. But once more the bogeys altered course toward the F-14s.

In peacetime, American pilots can fire their weapons at other aircraft only when attacked. In the past, that rule has meant that the adversary had to shoot first. But in an era when the first cut is often a fatal one, this rule of engagement has been reconsidered. In particular, an attack is presumed to be under way, even before a weapon has been fired, if a potentially hostile aircraft changes course five times to gain an offensive advantage.

Still beyond visual range, the Libyans matched the Americans' third attempt to intercept with another turn toward them, taking the encounter a step nearer the threshold of combat. At this point, the air warfare commander aboard the *Kennedy* radioed "Warning yellow. Weapons hold," ordering the Tomcats to prepare for action but to refrain from firing. The pilots flipped on all armament switches except for the master arm switch. The F-14s were just one toggle away from being ready to launch missiles.

As the American and Libyan planes snaked toward each other, each of the Tomcat pilots monitored his head-up display (HUD), which projects pertinent flight and weapons data onto a clear glass panel inside the wind-screen and allows the pilot to fly the aircraft without taking his eyes off the world outside. Three minutes into the engagement, following two more turns by the American planes, the lead Tomcat's RIO reported to his pilot and to the carrier: "The bogeys have jinked back at me again for the fifth time. They're on my nose now, inside of twenty miles. Master arm on."

The Libyans' behavior now qualified as an attack. The lead pilot's RIO began advising him where to steer the F-14 in order to position it for a missile launch. "Centering the T," he said, referring to the aiming symbol appearing on the HUD. As tension mounted, the pitch of his voice had risen. Its inflection had become more urgent.

The weapon of choice in this situation was the Sparrow missile, which homes on the target using reflections of the F-14's radar beam and can be launched from the front seat or the back. With his Sparrows armed and ready, the pilot radioed the carrier asking permission to launch. He received no reply to that transmission or to a second. The third was interrupted by his RIO calling "Fox one, fox one" and the sound of a Sparrow sprinting away from his Tomcat, followed by a curse from the pilot, who had not pulled the trigger. Ten seconds later another missile was launched. In the heat of the moment, his RIO may have forgotten to switch the Tomcat's radar from track-while-scan into the mode required for guiding the missiles. Both Sparrows flew wide of the mark.

Using customary tactics for such a situation, the Tomcats split up. Both bogeys turned toward the wingman, apparently following orders from the Libyan ground controller to single him out. By this time, the Americans could see the approaching jets as specks that quickly took the shape of MiG-23 Floggers. The wingman lined up the trailing MiG for a head-on shot and called "Fox one" as he triggered a Sparrow. The missile raced to the MiG, then exploded in a ball of red flame, blowing the airplane to pieces. "Good hit, good hit on one," radioed the flight leader, confirming his wingman's score. "Roger that, good kill, good kill!" came the response.

Meanwhile, the lead Tomcat was pursuing the other Flogger, turning sharply right, then left. Arriving at a firing position, the pilot found that he had slipped inside the Sparrow's minimum range of 3,000 feet. Switching his weapons selector to SW, he prepared to launch a Sidewinder.

"Shoot him," the RIO yelled to his pilot, encouraging him to launch the missile and be done with it. But instead of acting, the pilot shouted: "I can't. I don't have a tone!" He was referring to the noise that a Sidewinder transmits to the pilot's earphones when it senses a heat source. Then, suddenly the tone was there, a deafening growl that drowned out the intercom. The Flogger was in a shallow, descending turn to the left when the lead pilot pulled the trigger on his control stick. A split second later, the Sidewinder's rocket motor ignited, and the missile flew straight up the MiG's tailpipe. There was a small, bright flash surrounded by a puff of black smoke that extended into a spiral as the MiG nosed toward the sea.

"Good kill. Good kill," yelled the lead pilot, announcing the hit.

"Roger that," replied the wingman. "Two Floggers, two Floggers splashed. We're showing two good chutes in the air here."

Minutes later, having been relieved by other Tomcats launched from the *Kennedy*, Gypsy flight lurched to a halt on the deck of the carrier, and the four warriors aboard climbed down from their jets to a warm reception from everyone aboard.

The encounter between Tomcats and Floggers over the Mediterranean illustrates both the unchanging nature of aerial warfare and the phenomenal developments wrought by technology on a form of personal combat that is as old as the airplane itself. Were the fighter pilots of World War I alive today, they would discern a thread of continuity circling from their own exploits above the trenches of France in 1918 to the duel between American and Libyan pilots over the Gulf of Sidra seven decades later. Men like Baron von Richthofen and Eddie Rickenbacker might be awed by the sophistication of modern jet fighters and their weapons, but they would not be baffled. For they would understand that the dogfight remains a trial by combat in which the skill and determination of the pilots often decide the outcome, and where a single lapse may be fatal.

The air combat of today, however, is less a direct descendant of its World War I progenitor than the reinvention of it. In the late 1950s, at the dawn of the supersonic age, the one-on-one, close-in dogfight was officially decreed obsolete. The flying services of many nations reasoned that future air-to-air engagements would be fought with guided missiles launched from great distances, far beyond the range at which the eye of the pilot could discern the enemy. Acting on this conviction, the U.S. Navy commissioned (and the Air Force later adopted) the F-4 Phantom. Designed in the new idiom for air-superiority fighters, it lacked the quintessential weapon of the dogfight—a gun.

Air combat in Vietnam would reveal how premature was the idea of a standoff air battle. There were no front lines in the sky. That bogey out in front was more likely to be an American than a North Vietnamese. Under such conditions, launching a missile without eying the target was a formula for disaster.

At an airfield in Saudi Arabia, crewmen check the Sidewinder missiles of a U.S. Air Force F-15 poised to fly combat air patrol near the border of Iraq in August 1990. Mere hours after the Iraqi threat to Saudi oil fields became clear, squadrons of Eagles—the world's preeminent air-superiority fighter—began arriving from the United States to strengthen defenses.

The missiles themselves were a problem too. Far from being the "one shot, one kill" weapons promised, they often failed to find the target or, when they succeeded in that, did not explode. Even if a missile attack from long range were practical, many enemy planes could be counted on to survive.

Between the need to postpone firing until the target could be positively identified and the rate of missile failure, many an F-4 pilot unwillingly found himself in a close encounter with a North Vietnamese MiG. Often such confrontations brought him too near the foe to fire a missile, which requires several seconds to arm and begin homing on the target. Without a gun, he had little choice but to break off the engagement.

Influenced by these events, the theoreticians relented. Some later models of the F-4 were built with a 20-mm cannon aboard, and since then no air-superiority fighter designed in the United States has been built without a gun. However, loading a cannon and 1,200 rounds of ammunition into planes proved to be an incomplete solution, at least for U.S. pilots. Under the same theory that produced the gunless Phantom, nearly a generation of American fighter jockeys had been given incomplete training in air-combat maneuvering. To remedy this situation required not only intensive dogfight instruction early in a pilot's career, but more emphasis on dissimilar training—mock dogfighting against pilots flying enemy tactics in aircraft that could mimic the performance of enemy fighters.

Meanwhile, missiles gradually began to fulfill their original promise, as guidance systems and reliability improved. These weapons, so much better that they seemed almost new, proved themselves in the cauldron of the Middle East, where frequent air combat between Israel and its Arab neighbors proved that missiles could dominate air-to-air warfare when employed with tactics that played to their strengths.

Even so, the gun will remain a hallmark of the air-superiority fighter at least into the next generation of aircraft. The YF-23 and YF-22, prototypes of planes intended to take the U.S. Air Force into the next century, both have guns—as well as a host of technological innovations that promise to make them more agile, more powerful, and more lethal than ever before. ★

Rude Awakening in Southeast Asia

Mist swirls around a crew chief at Phan Rang air base in Vietnam as a Phantom pilot starts his engines for an early-morning mission. The F-4 was designed for the Navy in the late 1950s as an interceptor.

On April 4, 1965, a strike force of F-105 Thunderchief fighter-bombers took off from bases in Thailand and, escorted by F-100 fighters, crossed the Laotian panhandle into North Vietnam. The mission was to hit a bridge at Thanh Hoa with 750-pound bombs and AGM-12 Bullpup guided missiles, steered to the target with a small control stick manipulated by the F-105 pilot as he flew his own plane.

The bridge was an important target. Carrying the principal North Vietnamese rail and road arteries across the broad flood plain of the Song Ma River about seventy-five miles south of Hanoi, it was a vital link to the major port of Vinh and to the southern gateways of the Ho Chi Minh Trail.

As the strike force approached the target, four MiG-17s came out of nowhere, suddenly appearing high on the flanks of the bombers and their escort. The Air Force had no radar coverage of North Vietnam at that time, so there was no warning of the bandits. Two MiGs jumped the lead F-105 and his wingman in a slashing, diving, high-speed gun attack, and after completing the pass, all four dived away into the haze. The covering F-100s, armed with Sidewinder heat-seeking missiles and 20-mm cannon, got off a few snap shots as the MiGs flashed by, but they scored no kills. The toll for the mission, which left the bridge intact, was two F-105s destroyed, the first U.S. Air Force losses in air-to-air combat since the Korean War—all in all, an inauspicious opening round for the Americans.

The air war over North Vietnam had begun after the Gulf of Tonkin incident of August 2, 1964, in which North Vietnamese torpedo craft attacked a U.S. destroyer. In response, the Navy sent sixty-four aircraft to demolish these boats as well as their docks and supply facilities. The raid crippled the North's torpedo-boat flotilla. One A-4 Skyhawk fighter-bomber fell to enemy groundfire.

The first U.S. Air Force operations outside South Vietnam commenced the following December. Fighter-bombers flew armed reconnaissance missions against North Vietnamese supply routes—the Ho Chi Minh Trail—through northern Laos, code-named Barrel Roll. Pilots were authorized to seek and destroy so-called targets of opportunity—trucks, troop concentrations, boats, bridges, roads, and trails. As operations in Barrel Roll got under way, opposition consisted mainly of 37-mm antiaircraft artillery (AAA). This gun could reach as high as 20,000 feet, and though unas-

An F-105D Thunderchief, the workhorse of low- and medium-level bombing raids during the Vietnam War, heads north on a mission in April 1966. The single-seat fighter-bomber could fly 2,000 miles without refueling or carry a 12,000-pound bomb load. It was also armed with missiles and a 20-mm cannon. By the end of the war, F-105s had shot down more than two dozen MiGs.

sisted by radar aiming devices, it could be devastating to fighter-bombers flying low-level bombing or strafing passes.

Operation Rolling Thunder upped the ante in late March 1965 with the first Air Force strikes against the North Vietnamese panhandle. On the first several Rolling Thunder missions, AAA and machine-gun fire accounted for all American losses, so the dispatching of MiGs to defend the Thanh Hoa bridge heralded a significant rise in the danger to American pilots.

The United States was aware that thirty MiG-15s and MiG-17s had arrived at Phuc Yen, a recently completed air base near Hanoi, but intelligence analysts had discounted the threat they posed. Not only were these aircraft obsolescent, but the North Vietnamese pilots were believed to be inexperienced and poorly trained.

In a post-strike assessment, the Air Force confirmed that the North Vietnamese aircraft had taken off from Phuc Yen, only fifty miles from the target, as the American strike force crossed Laos. Following orders from controllers manning radars on the ground, the MiGs executed a classic "one pass and haul ass" operation. Hugging the deck, they snaked through the many valleys in that mountainous region, until they were perfectly positioned for a surprise intercept. Then, unseen by the Americans, they zoomed above the strike force and dived to attack. The MiGs returned immediately to the safety of their airfield. Under American rules of engagement in effect at the time, all such facilities were immune from attack as part of American strategy to increase pressure on the North gradually.

With MiGs now a force to be reckoned with, it became clear that the aged F-100s were of no help in protecting the F-105 Thunderchiefs. The F-100 had come into the U.S. Air Force inventory in 1955. It carried no radar other than a radar-ranging gunsight that could not detect a fighter more than a half mile away or one flying at a lower altitude. To intercept a MiG, an F-100 pilot needed assistance from a powerful radar on the ground, such as the North Vietnamese employed. Even then, the enemy planes would be undetectable until they began their climb to attack altitude, so any warning would come none too early. If an intercept occurred, the more maneuverable MiG might well escape or emerge victorious if the pilot chose to fight. Ultimately, F-100s were relegated mainly to a ground-support role in South Vietnam.

The F-105 Thunderchief—lovingly known to her pilots as the

Thud—had greater success against MiGs. The plane had been designed during the Cold War as a supersonic fighter-bomber for carrying a small nuclear bomb into Eastern Europe. Although it was never intended to be used as an air superiority dogfighter, the Thud had a radar that could detect an enemy plane at a distance of three miles. Furthermore, it carried a 20-mm Vulcan cannon—a six-barrel Gatling gun that could spew out 6,000 rounds a minute—as well as heat-seeking Sidewinder missiles. While the F-105 could not outturn the smaller, more agile MiGs, it was faster, especially at low altitude.

The Navy had an aging antidote for MiGs called the F-8 Crusader. Though out of production in 1965 and nearing retirement, the powerful and agile Crusader could catch up with and outmaneuver MiGs after their pass through a fighter-bomber formation. Crusader pilots operating from the Gulf of Tonkin downed eighteen MiGs at a cost of only four of their own.

Plans were afoot to even the odds against North Vietnam's MiGs. A new, better-equipped, and more maneuverable U.S. fighter had been built. EC-121s, the military version of the three-tail Lockheed Constellation airliner outfitted with powerful radar scanners were on the way. These planes would soon be patrolling off the coast of North Vietnam, detecting the MiGs as they became airborne and monitoring their course and altitude for the F-4s. But in the meantime, North Vietnam's Air Force would refine its tactics and continue to administer a costly drubbing to Americans sent north.

A Small Air Force with a Big Punch

The North Vietnamese pilots who shot down the F-105s near Thanh Hoa—and others like them who would continue to destroy or damage dozens of U.S. aircraft with comparatively few losses of their own—were scorned by most American aircrews who tangled with them. Most seemed to have just one trick in their bag: to sneak up from behind at a higher altitude and try to score while diving for the safety of their airfields. Few would pull out of that dive and return for a second pass.

Such behavior frustrated American fliers, who felt they were be-

Alongside a MiG-17, North Vietnamese ace Nguyen Van Bay demonstrates the tactics that reportedly earned him seven kills. Leather helmets were worn not only by Vietnamese MiG-17 pilots but by their Soviet and Chinese mentors as well, who recognized much later than the United States that fighter pilots needed the protection of crash helmets.

ing sniped at with little opportunity to even the balance sheet. Many blamed the U.S. rules of engagement that spared airfields in the North from attack. And although destroying the North Vietnamese Air Force (NVAF) on the ground would have reduced U.S. Navy and Air Force air-combat losses, doing so would also have hidden the inability of the American aviators to deal with the ostensibly minor threat posed by average pilots often flying outmoded aircraft according to predictable tactics.

For successes against marauding U.S. fighter-bombers and covering aircraft, the North Vietnamese Air Force was deeply indebted to the Soviet Union and to China for supplying fighters, devising tactics, and training the pilots. Learning the Soviet principles of air combat was an important part of the curriculum for the North Vietnamese student pilots. The Russians emphasized ground-control intercept (GCI) tactics, in which earthbound radar operators exercise strict control of individual fighter aircraft. Only the top flight-school graduates were given, upon their return to North Vietnam after their training, one of the North Vietnamese Air Force's handful of fighters.

North Vietnam relied primarily on two aircraft for air defense, the

1950s-vintage MiG-17 and the MiG-21, a much more modern and capable aircraft. The subsonic MiG-17 carried three cannons in the nose, one 37-mm and two 23-mm. Although the MiG-17 was capable of launching Alkali radar-guided missiles or Atoll heat seekers, the North Vietnamese rarely armed the fighter with such weapons. The same was true of supersonic MiG-21s, which began arriving in North Vietnam in December 1965, less than a year after the first Rolling Thunder sorties. Not until 1972 did MiG-21s outnumber MiG-17s in the inventory.

North Vietnamese fighter tactics were designed chiefly to disrupt attacking formations of American fighter-bombers and then to pick off straggling aircraft. With a mach 2.3 dash speed, a MiG-21 could intercept American fighter-bombers farther from the target than a MiG-17 given the same warning of the enemy's approach. Otherwise both of the aircraft were about equally suited to spooking the attacking planes.

To accomplish this, the MiGs attacked or feinted at the bomb-laden aircraft, prompting their pilots to jettison their ordnance before they reached the target. Rid of the weight and drag of perhaps more than a dozen bombs, each weighing up to 750 pounds, the planes were better able to defend themselves. Usually, however, the MiGs broke off the attack as soon as their pilots saw the bombs tumbling down.

This stratagem worked quite well. On days when MiGs were airborne—and in the early stages of the war, that was only a couple of times a week—more than half of the bombs that were intended for military targets were dumped relatively harmlessly on the North Vietnamese countryside. Moreover, American fliers unintentionally aided the enemy in achieving their goal. Fearful of being shot down and more than eager to tangle with their antagonists, they often jettisoned their bombs at the mere appearance of MiGs in the sky. To put a stop to the waste, the U.S. Air Force ordered each of its pilots not to jettison his payload unless his own aircraft was threatened.

Attacks on U.S. fighters flying MiGCAP—a combat air patrol mission to protect the strike force against MiGs—were riskier for the North Vietnamese, inasmuch as CAP pilots had no more important duty than to shoot down any enemy aircraft that came within reach. But North Vietnamese aviators quickly learned to pounce as the Americans departed the target area. At this point,

During a dogfight in December 1966, a MiG-21 streaks above the North Vietnamese landscape near Hanoi. With excellent maneuverability and mach 2.3 speed, the MiG-21 was a daunting opponent. It supplemented its cannons with heat-seeking missiles—a pair of Soviet-made Atolls, similar in size to Sidewinders, that were carried under the delta wings.

with their fuel tanks nearly empty, the planes could not afford to engage in gas-guzzling combat maneuvers.

No tactics are infallible, however, and occasionally a North Vietnamese pilot would be unable to escape a dogfight. Even more rarely, he might initiate one. In these circumstances, a pilot in a MiG-17 could be as much of a challenge as one flying a MiG-21. The older plane, though much slower than U.S. fighters, could turn tighter, especially at low altitudes and when traveling at speeds less than 450 knots, a common occurrence in air combat. The MiG-21 could not only keep up with American planes, it could also outturn them in the thinner atmosphere above 20,000 feet.

Yet for several reasons, North Vietnamese pilots won few of these encounters. Trained to follow orders from the ground, these fliers were little more than radio-controlled guidance systems for a maneuvering surface-to-air weapons platform. Almost to a man, they were neither very skilled nor very imaginative in tossing their airplanes about the sky. American pilots knew how to overcome the maneuvering advantage of the MiGs by abandoning a simple, level, turning pursuit in favor of climbs and dives to achieve a firing position *(pages 54-67)*. Few North Vietnamese pilots could defend themselves against these maneuvers, and fewer still could duplicate them.

Neither were the MiG pilots schooled in flight integrity, the art of mutual support in a hassle. If several MiGs were vectored to an American formation and one was singled out for attack, the rest would abandon him. By contrast, American pilots always flew in pairs or larger groups so that one pilot would be in a position to look out for another.

Furthermore, most North Vietnamese pilots proved to be inferior marksmen. To score a kill with a cannon—the MiGs' predominant weapon—the gun must be trained on the spot where projectile and target will collide. Without a radar-tracking gunsight to establish an aiming point, getting a hit when both aircraft are moving and

Three commemorative stamps issued by North Vietnam early in the conflict exaggerate the destruction of U.S. planes by MiGs, antiaircraft artillery, and small-arms fire. The top stamp claims a toll of 2,500 aircraft, nearly as many as were lost during the entire war.

jinking at several hundred miles an hour requires more highly developed air-combat maneuvering skills than most North Vietnamese aviators possessed.

For all these shortcomings, however, the first man in the air war over Vietnam to score five kills and become an ace was a North Vietnamese pilot, Captain Nguyen Van Bay. Flying a MiG-17, Captain Nguyen had shot down seven American fighters by May 1966.

Four other North Vietnamese Air Force fliers would claim this coveted status within two years. One was the highest-scoring ace of the war on either side. His name was Colonel Tomb, and he amassed thirteen victories. Strangely, the North Vietnamese government never publicized any of Tomb's victories—something they did for every other North Vietnamese ace. For that reason—and because it was difficult to imagine a Vietnamese flier capable of such a feat—many American aviators concluded that he and a few other outstanding fighter pilots must have been foreigners. Some even surmised that Colonel Tomb was a composite of several Chinese, North Korean, or even Soviet pilots, who together scored this baker's dozen and whose identities could not be publicized for reasons of diplomacy.

A New Menace in the Skies over Hanoi

Taking stock of an aging inventory of carrier-based attack aircraft not long after the Korean War, the U.S. Navy made plans for the future. Technological breakthroughs—air-to-air guided missiles, on-board target acquisition radar, and sophisticated guidance systems—seemed to portend a revolution in aerial warfare. A revolutionary aircraft was called for to maintain the superiority of the Navy's primary strike force, the carrier battle group.

To address the situation, the Navy commissioned the design of a twin-engine strike aircraft. Then, after work had begun in 1954, the Navy changed the requirement to a missile fighter. Oddly enough, the melding of these two disparate criteria resulted in a superb aircraft. Designated the F-4 Phantom, the multipurpose jet entered Navy service in 1961; the Air Force started buying Phantoms in 1962. Noisy and smoky, the F-4 was not particularly phantomlike, but at the time —and for the rest of the decade thereafter—it was the premier airplane in its class, holding world records in speed, altitude, and rate of climb.

The Phantom carried a two-man crew, one to fly the plane and another, seated behind him, whose primary responsibilities were to operate a powerful, long-range acquisition radar installed in the aircraft. The Navy called the backseater a radar intercept officer (RIO). At first, the Air Force used a pilot as the second crew member to operate flight controls in the back seat. This feature, like two engines, provided a greater margin of safety in combat. But putting the controls of a high-performance aircraft in two pairs of hands was soon recognized as a mistake. Delicate egos were bruised—only one man could fly the aircraft—and it proved uneconomical to train backseaters as pilots. The Air Force soon stopped the practice. The second set of controls in the F-4, though retained in later models, became superfluous, and the backseater, no longer a pilot, became known as the weapons systems officer, or WSO. Besides working the radar, the WSO programmed the plane's inertial navigation system, which senses aircraft motion and uses a computer to calculate direction and distance traveled. Whatever the backseater's title or duties, everyone agreed that, in combat, two pairs of eyes were far better than one.

In keeping with its original function as an interceptor, the F-4 was equipped with Sparrow radar-guided missiles having a thirteen-mile range and heat-seeking Sidewinders for use at distances up to two miles. The experts held that the F-4 could pick off most hostile aircraft with Sparrows before they came into view. Any enemy planes that survived the Sparrow attack would succumb a few min-

In full war paint, the two-seat F-4-Phantom presented a vision of lethality in the skies over Vietnam. Carrying as many as twelve 750-pound bombs as an attack aircraft, it was also America's premier dogfighter. The E model had a 20-mm cannon protruding below the nose that could fire 6,000 rounds a minute. The plane also carried four radar-homing Sparrow air-to-air missiles and an equal number of infrared-guided Sidewinders.

utes later to Sidewinders. So bewitching was this logic of the missiles that the Phantom, alone among fighters, did not carry a gun. Even though the missiles were useless at ranges less than 1,000 feet (they needed the distance to begin homing on a target), those in charge of building the Phantom were convinced that close-in dogfighting was dead and that guns, never a very accurate weapon, had outlived their usefulness in air combat.

The war in Vietnam would prove this theory premature. When the F-4 first tasted combat there, U.S. rules of engagement required visual identification of a target as an enemy aircraft before firing at it. The practice made sense, inasmuch as most of the planes in the sky were American, but it also negated the standoff capability of the Sparrow missile. Later in the war, Phantoms would be equipped with special radar receivers developed under a program called Combat Tree. These electronics enabled RIOs and WSOs to recognize MiGs on their radarscopes from signals that were used to identify North Vietnamese fighters to their ground controllers and make it safe for the Americans to employ Sparrows out to their thirteen-mile maximum range.

But until the arrival of Combat Tree, a Phantom pilot typically had to approach within visual range of a MiG to be certain of his target. And then he could not be certain of his weapons. Failures in the missiles themselves, glitches in weapons-system circuitry aboard the aircraft, or a propensity among aviators to launch at targets that were beyond the missiles' capabilities to intercept caused fully 90 percent of the Sparrows and 50 percent of the Sidewinders fired during the first three years of the Phantom's combat to miss the target.

Thus, once an enemy aircraft was close enough to be seen, a dogfight often developed where the gunless Phantoms were handicapped. "I loved the F-4 and thought it was probably the answer to a fighter pilot's prayers—with the exception of the lack of an internal gun. We missed that terribly," said William Kirk, an Air Force major who flew Phantoms over North Vietnam.

In one melee above Hanoi, Kirk was in a good position to fire a Sidewinder at a MiG-17 when two Phantoms cut between him and his target. He dared not launch, since the missile would track the strongest heat source in its field of view. By the time his squadronmates had cleared out, Kirk found himself inside the Sidewinder's minimum range but perfectly set up for a gun attack. The MiG got away. Said Kirk, "We could engage at will, but we lacked the ordnance to knock them down. We had no guns."

Another source of frustration was the tendency of early Sidewinder missiles to lock onto heat sources other than the intended target. "There I was," said Kirk, describing another encounter, "closing at a Godawful rate with Sidewinders in an overhead attack. I'm pointing those Sidewinders at the ground and they are just growling and sputtering like mad. Of course, all they are 'seeing' is the heat of the ground."

Experiences like Kirk's, repeated many times, convinced the Air Force that the Phantom needed a gun. The first model to get one was the F-4D, which began arriving in Vietnam in May 1967. Its weapons system was modified to accommodate a Vulcan 20-mm cannon mounted in a pod hung from the belly. Later, in the F-4E Phantom (pages 34-35), designers would rework the nose of the aircraft so that it could carry the cannon internally.

Kirk remained in Southeast Asia long enough to experience the difference a gun could make. Piloting an F-4D on October 24, 1967, Kirk led Buick flight and two other four-plane formations. Their assignment was to fly MiGCAP, protecting the strike force of Thunderchiefs against North Vietnamese MiGs. The fighters worked closely with Disco, call sign for an EC-121 warning aircraft orbiting over Laos, and Red Crown, a Navy cruiser in the Gulf of Tonkin. Both provided radar coverage of North Vietnam, informing pilots of MiG takeoffs and movements.

"There was a lot of chatter on the strike frequency," Kirk remembered. "I was having a tough time picking up calls from Red Crown and Disco. I did get the call that mattered, though. It came through loud and clear. 'Buick, he's at five o'clock, five miles, and he's attacking you.' "

Kirk ordered his flight into a 180-degree turn, while the other Phantoms continued with the bombers. "As I rolled out of this turn," said Kirk, "I met a MiG-21 head-on. It was highly polished—a beautiful little airplane—and as we passed within twenty yards of each other, I thought 'What a shame to have to shoot at him.' " His second thought was that he had let the MiGs get through his protective screen, and now they would go after the bombers.

"I pulled up into the vertical, turning right to reverse, looked back and was amazed to see that the MiG was doing the same thing. They never got into turning fights, and yet this guy was trying to match my turn. He would have been a lot better off to go and fire his missiles at the 105s, because I was really no threat to him. If he had gone on, there was no way I could have caught him."

As the planes chased each other like cars on a high-speed Ferris wheel, neither pilot could gain an edge over the other. Kirk's Phantom still carried wing tanks, which he decided to rid himself of to reduce weight and drag. "As I bottomed out of the second turn, I was frantically trying to find the outboard jettison switch without taking my eyes off the MiG. I finally found it, and as I pulled up into him, with him diving down the opposite side of the circle, I blew my tanks off. The tanks were still full of fuel, so when they came off, they were streaming fuel as they tumbled down behind me. I don't know if that confused him or if he thought the tanks were me or what, but he rolled out of his turn and headed for the tanks—just for an instant, which was long enough to give me an advantage. Now I was a threat to him. He panicked. The MiG-21 has real poor visibility in the rear quadrant and he started jinking so that he could keep an eye on me." Despite the maneuvering, Kirk's backseater got a missile lock-on, and the pilot fired a Sparrow. It tracked well but exploded about twenty-five feet behind the MiG, causing little if any damage.

Now closing rapidly on his target, Kirk was about to confirm the wisdom of equipping the Phantom with a gun. First, however, he had to look inside the cockpit for a moment to bring the Vulcan on line. "There were two switches on the pedestal in front of the stick to flip," recalled Kirk. "It couldn't have taken more than a couple of seconds, but when I looked up, I had a wind-screen full of MiG-21! He was in a hard left turn and the gunsight pipper was right in the middle of his back. I squeezed the trigger and the 20-mm Gatling gun sawed a hole right through him between the wing roots. He bailed out immediately."

Operation Bolo—a Masterly Deceit

Colonel Robin Olds stiffened in the front seat of his F-4C as he listened to the intercom report of his backseater, First Lieutenant Chuck Clifton. Unseen except on the plane's radarscope, a bogey was closing fast at twelve o'clock low. The curtain was rising on Operation Bolo. By the end of the day, the pilots of Olds's Eighth Tactical Fighter Wing would compile a record of MiG kills that, at the end of the Vietnam War, would stand unmatched as the Americans' best showing against the North Vietnamese Air Force. Ironically, this win, preceding as it did the appearance of gun-toting Phantoms in Southeast Asia by several months, would be achieved by missiles alone. And it would be a classic demonstration of the air-combat axiom that there is no such thing as cheating. Victory by fraud or deceit is as glorious as any other.

The North Vietnamese Air Force had been especially active against American strike forces in the latter part of 1966, and U.S. fighter pilots were thoroughly frustrated. The MiGs now operated out of six airfields, all of which would enjoy immunity from attack by American forces for several more months. When the F-105 Thuds penetrated North Vietnamese airspace, the MiGs would scramble to intercept, but seldom could American fighters flying MiGCAP draw them into an aerial duel. At the sight of F-4s, the MiGs fled. The U.S. Air Force decided that something bold and unexpected was called for. "We gave the job to the man most likely to succeed," recalled an Air Force general. "We gave it to Olds, of course."

This remarkable officer was as handsome, virile, and dashing as the newspapers described him. Sporting a bushy mustache, the forty-five-year-old aviator was the epitome of the cocky American fighter pilot. An all-American tackle and football-team captain at West Point, he already had a distinguished career behind him. Flying P-38s and P-51s in World War II, he had shot down twelve Germans. Promoted to full colonel at the tender age of thirty, Olds was a founding member of the Air Force's first jet aerobatic team and in 1948 took command of a Royal Air Force squadron, the first foreigner ever to do so. His abilities as a fighter pilot were unsurpassed. Throughout his career, whether in the field or at headquarters, he had always had a job related to fighters, specializing in operations, plans, and tactics.

While he was based in California, Olds met 1940s motion picture star Ella Raines and impressed her with his fighter-pilot panache. He invited her to an airshow at the base and disappeared. She thought she had been deserted. Then somebody told her he was flying one of the aircraft in a thrilling aerobatic demonstration for the crowd.

They were married, and she accompanied him as he moved frequently between stateside and overseas assignments—though not to Ubon, Thailand, where he took charge of the Eighth Tactical Fighter Wing (TFW) in September 1966. Old enough to be the father of his youngest pilots, he inspired them by example (he could fly with the best of them) as well as by his formidable reputation. But for the challenge of coming up with something "bold and unexpected" for the North Vietnamese, his tactical genius was more valuable than his stick-and-rudder skills.

Setting to the task with enthusiasm, Colonel Olds devised a plan for a large-scale fighter sweep that would capitalize on North Vietnamese Air Force tactics against the Rolling Thunder bombing missions that had been pounding the North for twenty-two months. The formations for

Colonel Robin Olds, commander of the Eighth Tactical Fighter Wing, is borne aloft by his pilots after completing his hundredth combat mission over North Vietnam on September 23, 1967—the last of his yearlong tour in Vietnam. Under Olds, the wing downed twenty-four MiG-17s and MiG-21s, a record of victories that would go unmatched during the war.

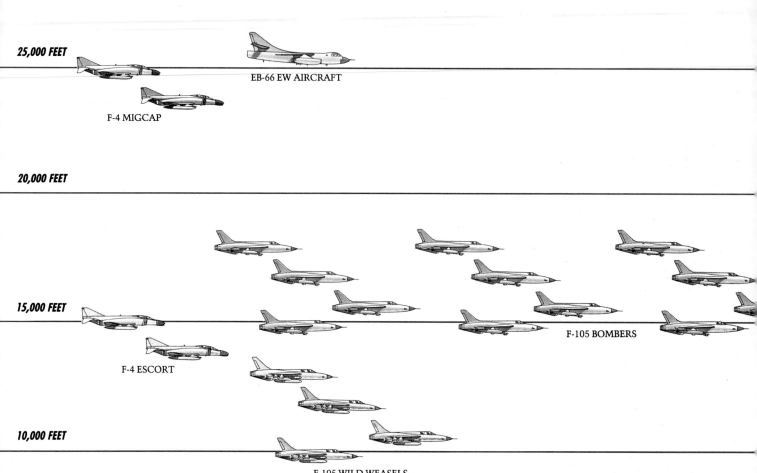

25,000 FEET

EB-66 EW AIRCRAFT

F-4 MIGCAP

20,000 FEET

15,000 FEET

F-105 BOMBERS

F-4 ESCORT

10,000 FEET

F-105 WILD WEASELS

these missions gave Olds the idea of a MiG-killing mission that would depend on a ruse to lure the enemy planes into a fight they could not run away from. Since the MiGs preferred to go after the heavily laden F-105 fighter-bombers, Olds planned to trick North Vietnamese ground-control intercept operators into believing his Phantoms were Thuds. To do this, his fighter wing had to mimic a bombing attack in every detail. The idea was not an Olds original. Several months earlier, a flight of Air Force F-4s had fooled two MiG-17s into thinking they were bombers and shot them down. But as yet, no one had tried the ruse on the scale that Olds had in mind.

By December, he had formulated the blueprint for Operation Bolo. The Bolo pilots—Olds's men plus others from the 366th Tactical Fighter Wing based at Da Nang, South Vietnam—would fly the same routes at the same altitude and airspeed as F-105s did on a normal bombing mission. The F-4s planned also to adopt the radio call signs and communications procedures that were customarily used by the Thuds. Even takeoff times and rendezvous over target were the same. Olds's planes were specially outfitted for this mission with electronic countermeasures (ECM) pods, which were usually carried only by the fighter-bombers. The overall effect was to make them look exactly like F-105s on the North Vietnamese ra-

The heart of a typical Rolling Thunder bombing mission against North Vietnam was a strike force of sixteen F-105 bombers, each with radar-jamming equipment that produced overlapping signals on enemy scopes and made individual targeting by SAMs difficult. A few thousand feet lower, two flights of F-105 Wild Weasels, one ahead of the strike force and the other positioned below the last flight to cover the withdrawal, attacked SAM radars with Shrike missiles. About ten miles in front, F-4 Phantoms flew top cover—MiG-CAP—for the bombers; the rear was escorted by other F-4s flying about three miles behind the strike force. At 25,000 feet, two EB-66 electronic warfare (EW) aircraft—each protected from MiGs by F-4s—jammed North Vietnamese radars with high-intensity emissions.

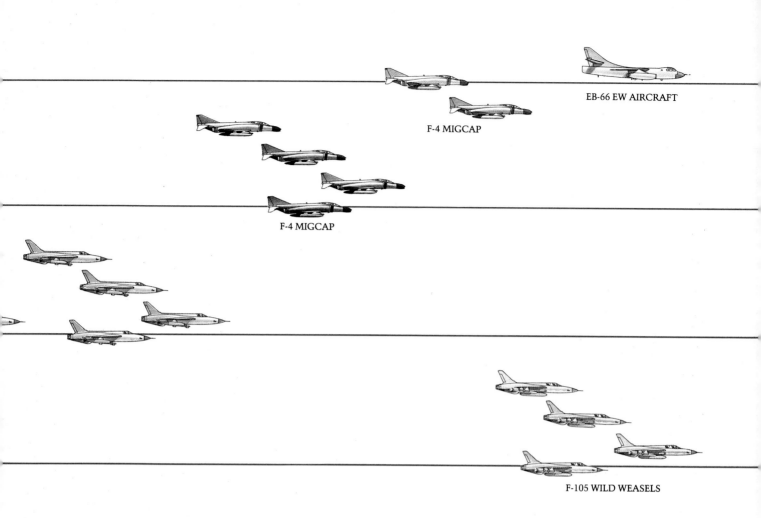

EB-66 EW AIRCRAFT

F-4 MIGCAP

F-4 MIGCAP

F-105 WILD WEASELS

darscopes. To complete the deception, there would be the usual bevy of support aircraft for a Rolling Thunder strike package, almost a hundred planes in all.

A thick cloud layer obscured Phuc Yen air base as the Phantoms approached. But similar weather on other days had not discouraged MiGs from making a pass at a Rolling Thunder strike force. Like an angler trolling for bass, Olds led the F-4s right over Phuc Yen. About fifteen miles past the airfield, he executed a 180-degree turn and brought the group back. Then he got a nibble, as MiG-21s began popping up through the cloud cover.

The MiG that Olds's backseater now alerted him to had not yet emerged above the clouds but had passed beneath the flight going in the opposite direction. It was probably being vectored by ground control intercept operators into position for a stern attack. Three more bogeys were spotted, closing rapidly, and the battle was joined. Swinging left toward the enemy fighters, Olds fired two Sparrows at one of the MiGs, but both missiles failed to track. He then launched two Sidewinders, but they guided toward the heat of the undercast, and the targeted MiG escaped destruction. It was an inauspicious beginning, and more MiGs were appearing from "all around the clock."

Then Olds's wingman achieved a boresight lock-on. In boresight mode, the F-4's radar antenna, upon which a Sparrow missile depends for guidance, is pointed straight ahead. The pilot, not the WSO, determines where the radar is aimed by steering the airplane. In this instance, the pilot centered the radarscope steering dot on the MiG and salvoed two Sparrows. One of them malfunctioned, but the other went true, exploding just forward of the target's tail. The MiG-21 flew on for an instant, then cartwheeled, spewing large pieces of tail in its wake. Trailing black smoke, it went into a sluggish, flat spin and disappeared into the cloud deck below. The score was now one to nothing.

A brief minute later, another F-4 obtained a weak Sidewinder tone on a MiG that was trying to sneak up behind a member of Olds's flight. To boost the heat-seeking missile's chance for a kill, the pilot closed the distance at full throttle. When the tone was strong and steady, he squeezed the firing button and the Sidewinder leaped off the rails straight to the target, scoring a solid hit behind the wing. Two down.

One MiG burst through the undercast into position right on Olds's tail. Olds broke hard left to throw off the MiG's aim and in so doing spotted another MiG flying across his nose in a steep left turn. He knew his F-4 could not match the MiG-21 in a horizontal turning contest, and so he began a textbook demonstration of using the vertical plane to overcome an opponent's edge in maneuverability. He pulled back hard on the stick, climbing above the MiG's flight path. At the top he flipped over to his right, away from the MiG, in a barrel roll that put him in an inverted descent cutting inside the track of the MiG's horizontal turn. As he righted himself at the bottom of the loop he was in good position for a shot from below and behind the MiG.

Olds believes that the enemy pilot never saw the F-4 on his tail. "We were at his seven o'clock position at about .95 mach. Range was 4,500 feet. The MiG obligingly pulled up well above the horizon. He was exactly downsun. I put the aiming pipper on his tailpipe, heard a perfect Sidewinder growl in my headset, squeezed the trigger, hesitated and squeezed it once again.

"The first missile went slightly down, then arced gracefully up, heading for impact. The second missile appeared to track perfectly also. Suddenly, the MiG-21 erupted in a brilliant flash of orange flame. The whole wing separated from the fuselage and flew back

One of the most deadly threats to U.S. aircraft in Vietnam was the Soviet-made SA-2 surface-to-air missile (SAM). Guided by radar, it could rise to 60,000 feet at more than three times the speed of sound to maim or destroy a plane with its 349-pound warhead. When a strike force of bombers headed into North Vietnam on a raid, the job of SAM suppression fell primarily to specialized two-seat F-105 Thunderchiefs called Wild Weasels.

Major Leo Thorsness was a Wild Weasel pilot. On April 19, 1967, he and his back-seater, Captain Harold Johnson, led a flight of four F-105 Wild Weasels clearing a path to the Xuan Mai army base, thirty miles southwest of Hanoi in a targeting area known as Route Pack Six. Approaching the target area, Thorsness picked up a strong signal from a SAM site and fired a radar-seeking Shrike missile. It dived away into the haze, and moments later the SAM radar ceased transmitting. Thorsness and his wingman then proceeded to obliterate another SAM site with cluster bombs—then suddenly found themselves in a blizzard of antiaircraft fire. The second F-105 was hit, and its crew ejected. Circling as the parachutes floated to earth, Thorsness summoned rescue helicopters. But before the chutes touched the ground, a MiG-17 approached. He blew the plane from the sky with his cannon.

Now short on fuel, Thorsness rendezvoused with a KC-135 tanker orbiting over Laos, then returned to Xuan Mai to shield the rescue team, now menaced by three MiGs. He scattered them with his remaining 500 rounds. When four more MiGs appeared, he led them on a twisting chase through mountain passes, then returned to the rescue scene—stingless, but a threatening presence—until other F-105s arrived. Then, almost out of fuel, he headed for base, landing as his tanks went dry.

Just eleven days later—and only seven missions from going home—Thorsness and Johnson were shot down and captured. Upon release in 1973, Thorsness was awarded the Medal of Honor *(above, left)* for his role in the deliverance of those fliers one spring day six years earlier.

in the airstream, together with a mass of smaller debris. The MiG swapped ends immediately, and tumbled forward for a few instants. It then fell, twisting, corkscrewing, tumbling lazily toward the top of the clouds. There was no pilot ejection before it entered the undercast." The wing commander's score made three.

At this point, Olds's four-ship flight, the first to arrive over the target, was low on fuel and had to withdraw. Flights arriving in the fake bomber stream a few minutes later took over and continued the battle, ambushing another MiG from the six o'clock position and knocking it out of the sky with a Sidewinder. Next, a flight of four more MiG-21s, trailed by two others, was spotted. Phantoms downed three of the enemy fighters in quick succession with Sparrow missiles.

With the final tally for the day seven MiGs destroyed and not a single American aircraft lost, Operation Bolo was a smashing success. Although more MiG-21s were in crates at Phuc Yen, ready to be assembled, nearly half of the North Vietnamese Air Force's operational MiG-21 force had been wiped out with one stinging blow. Of course, a mission of this sort, which relied so heavily on deception, could not often be repeated. Nevertheless, Operation Bolo had provided a much-needed boost for American fighter pilots' morale. As Olds told reporters after the battle, "We outflew, outshot, and outfought them."

Exchange Rates in the Currency of Dogfighting

On March 31, 1968, fifteen months after Operation Bolo, President Lyndon B. Johnson offered the North Vietnamese an olive branch by halting Rolling Thunder air raids north of the twentieth parallel. The pause gave American military strategists an opportunity to evaluate three years' air combat over North Vietnam.

The results were sobering. The U.S. Navy had shot down 3.7 MiGs for every fighter lost; the Air Force's kill ratio was about the same, 3 to 1. Both figures compared poorly to the kill ratio achieved during the Korean War, where American pilots had outscored the opposition 10 to 1. And while no American had yet shot down five enemy aircraft to become an ace, several pilots in the North Vietnamese Air Force had achieved that status.

The Navy jumped out in front of the Air Force in addressing this problem. It asked Captain Frank W. Ault, an experienced fighter pilot and aircraft-carrier skipper, to analyze aerial engagements in Southeast Asia and suggest ways to improve the Navy's kill ratio. His findings, published as the "Ault Report" in early 1969, listed 242 recommendations. One of them pierced right to the heart of the problem that had plagued American fighter pilots from the outset of the war. Expected to prevail with missiles fired from a distance, they had received almost no training in air-combat maneuvering, the art of the dogfight. These flying skills, Ault contended, were just as crucial in the supersonic age as they had been in the days of wood-and-fabric biplanes.

Responding to this argument, the Navy established a fighter weapons school—now known as Top Gun—at Miramar Naval Air Station in California. Its purpose was to sharpen the air-combat skills of naval aviators through classroom study and aerial workouts that pitted students flying F-4s against instructors in older U.S. aircraft comparable in performance to MiGs. Such exercises, known as dissimilar aircraft training, would lead to a substantial leap in the Navy kill ratio and help make naval aviators the first aces of the Vietnam War.

The Air Force nine years earlier had established a fighter weapons school at Nellis Air Force Base in Nevada. From its own analysis of air combat over North Vietnam, the Air Force also decided to increase the amount and the level of schooling in air-combat maneuvering. At Nellis, however, students and instructors alike flew jets with similar performance envelopes, with the result that Air Force pilots sent to Southeast Asia had no more idea than their predecessors of how best to fight North Vietnam's obsolescent, but highly maneuverable, aircraft.

Meanwhile, peace talks in Paris dragged on desultorily. To U.S. negotiators, the North Vietnamese appeared to regard the bombing halt less as a step toward peace than as an opportunity to improve air defenses and add to their inventory of fighters. On April 6, 1972, after forty-two months of fruitless discussions, and confronted by evidence that the North's forces were preparing new offensives against the U.S. and South Vietnamese forces, President Richard M. Nixon ordered the resumption of bombing strikes. Once again,

The Air-to-Air Arsenal

In combat, a fighter pilot has four types of weapons at his fingertips. For close-in duels at ranges of 2,000 feet or less, his choice is almost necessarily the cannon. Missiles are useless here; some must fly as far as 3,000 feet before they begin to home on the target.

Beyond effective cannon range, a pilot will plan a missile attack. Whether to shoot an infrared (IR) missile that senses heat emitted by the quarry or a radar-guided weapon that homes on electromagnetic en- ergy reflected from the target depends on the distance at which a target can be detected and whether the missile has sufficient fuel and speed to reach it.

The diagram at right shows typical ranges at which heat-seeking and radar-guided missiles are launched from behind a target. Optimum conditions—the common circumstance of two fighters roaring directly toward each other, for example—can more than triple these distances.

A predetermined course. Cannon shells follow a flight path that cannot be altered after the rounds leave the gun. To increase the probability of a kill, a pilot prefers a position behind his opponent. A gunsight linked to a target-tracking radar shows the pilot where to point his gun so that the projectiles will intercept it.

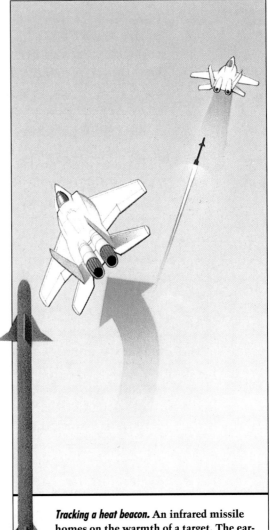

Tracking a heat beacon. An infrared missile homes on the warmth of a target. The earliest of these devices had to be fired from behind an adversary; their detectors could track nothing cooler than fully exposed engine exhaust. Keener models have been developed; they can pick up the exhaust plume from the side or even head-on.

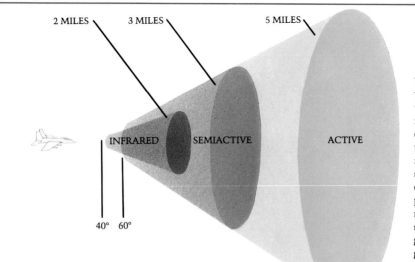

2 MILES 3 MILES 5 MILES

INFRARED SEMIACTIVE ACTIVE

40° 60°

The conical shapes at left show where a target can expect to be threatened by three kinds of missiles. The angle of the cone depends on the field of view of the guidance system. An infrared missile can track a heat source within forty degrees or so of the direction the weapon is pointed. Semiactive and active radar homing cover a cone of sixty degrees or so, with actively guided weapons having the greater range because of the self-sufficient guidance system.

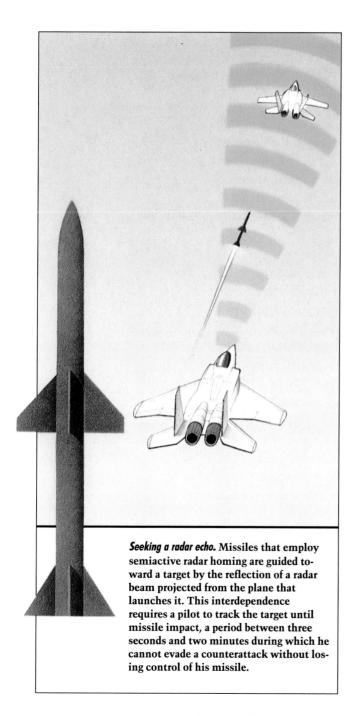

Seeking a radar echo. Missiles that employ semiactive radar homing are guided toward a target by the reflection of a radar beam projected from the plane that launches it. This interdependence requires a pilot to track the target until missile impact, a period between three seconds and two minutes during which he cannot evade a counterattack without losing control of his missile.

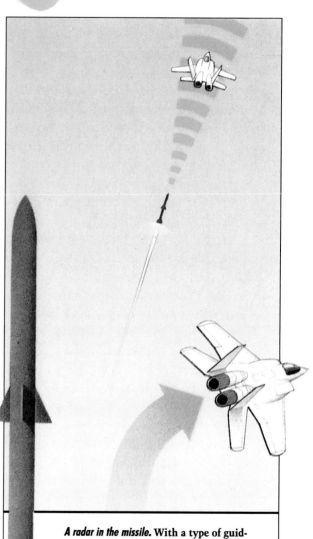

A radar in the missile. With a type of guidance called active homing, a radar transmitter aboard the missile is activated after launch, illuminating the target. The missile then homes on reflections of its own radar beam. This system—also known as launch-and-leave—frees a pilot to engage another target or take evasive action as soon as he shoots.

Navy pilots from aircraft carriers steaming in the Gulf of Tonkin and Air Force pilots based mostly in Thailand took off to do battle in the skies above Hanoi.

Navy Lieutenant Randy "Duke" Cunningham was an F-4 pilot aboard the USS *Constellation* when orders came to renew the air assault against North Vietnam. One of the early graduates of Top Gun, Cunningham was a prime example of the Navy's new, post-bombing-halt outlook. His mentors had been the small cadre of Navy aviators who had never forsaken air-combat maneuvering. Cunningham soaked up every bit of wisdom they could bestow.

From time to time during the bombing pause, Cunningham had managed to get ashore, where he met several Air Force Phantom pilots. Invariably, they pumped him for information. Hanging on his words, they amazed him by taking notes as he talked aerial tactics. One squadron commander asked how the Air Force could improve its tactics. Cunningham, Navy to the core, replied that the solution was to put blue-water pilots in their planes.

On January 19, 1972, Cunningham got the chance to put his skills to use. He and his radar intercept officer, Lieutenant (junior grade) Willie Driscoll, were flying MiGCAP for a photoreconnaissance mission to determine how many MiGs had moved into a new North Vietnamese air base at Quang Lang, south of Hanoi. On a previous foray into the area, the North Vietnamese had not fired on the Navy airplanes, but this time was different. Antiaircraft artillery opened up on the reconnaissance bird, and an A-6 Intruder strike aircraft responded by rolling in to bomb them. Cunningham decided to place his flight between Quang Lang and a neighboring MiG base at Bai Thuong, known to have sent MiGs aloft earlier.

Unfortunately, in taking this position, Cunningham placed the MiGCAP within range of an SA-2 SAM site. The F-4s were forced to evade no fewer than eighteen missiles in the next few minutes. The sky was clear, so Cunningham could see the puff of dust and exhaust gases raised as the missile launched. One tactic for evading an SA-2 was to dive toward it. As the plane dropped below the SAM, the missile would nose over in pursuit. Seeing this maneuver through the top of the canopy, the F-4 pilot would then pull up hard. Done properly, with the SAM close in, the missile would be unable to turn sharply enough to follow. Cunningham eluded two SAMs with this stratagem, then watched another rocket pass less than 100 feet from his wingman's plane—close enough to activate the SA-2's proximity fuze, which would detonate the warhead if the missile passed within several hundred feet of the target. This SA-2 must have been defective, because it did not explode.

Cunningham then spotted two aircraft. At first he thought they were American A-7 ground-attack planes, but then he noticed flames from their afterburners and knew that the airplanes were MiG-21s. The A-7 has no afterburner. He dived at 600 knots to get on one MiG's tail, and RIO Driscoll locked his radar onto the target. The radar provided tracking information for the Sparrow missiles under the fuselage. "Go boresight!" yelled Cunningham to Driscoll, telling the RIO to point the F-4's radar antenna straight ahead so that Cunningham could aim the radar at the MiG as he maneuvered. "They're locked up," Driscoll objected, telling the pilot the radar had already acquired the target. "Shoot! Shoot! Shoot!"

But Cunningham had second thoughts. Frustrated by the Sparrow in training against drone targets, he was loath to trust the capricious radar-guided missile now that he had a real target in his sights. Instead, he flicked the firing switch on his control stick to SW—Sidewinder. Cunningham had no other option; his squadron was still flying the Navy's gunless F-4Js. He heard in his headset the familiar tone emitted by the missile's infrared-seeker head, which was already locked onto the target's hot exhaust. Cunningham slipped into position behind the MiG and launched. The enemy pilot must have realized the danger, for at that instant he broke hard right—still in afterburner—and evaded the missile.

Instead of following the tighter-turning MiG-21, Cunningham applied a lesson learned flying against planes of similar performance at Top Gun. He rolled the other way into a descending turn. By opening the distance between himself and his quarry, he hoped for a shot from below and behind the MiG. During the turn, he saw the MiG's wingman retreat.

Now Cunningham was at treetop level, doing 600 knots. The MiG pilot must have lost sight of the F-4 because he banked to the left—straight into Cunningham's sights at perfect Sidewinder range—3,000 feet directly behind the MiG. Cunningham squeezed the trigger on the stick and saw the Sidewinder leap ahead. The missile blew the MiG's entire tail away. This was the Navy's first MiG kill in twenty-one months—and a cause for celebration when he and Driscoll returned to the Constellation.

Cunningham and Driscoll got their second kill, a MiG-17, on May 8. This fight began when the MiG latched onto Cunningham's wingman in the six o'clock position and fired an Atoll heat-seeking missile. Cunningham radioed a warning to his wingman, who turned sharply. The missile could not "make the corner," and wandered off harmlessly. Cunningham charged after the MiG, firing a Sidewinder from an angle that usually required too tight a turn of the missile to reach the target. This time, however, the Sidewinder curved gracefully toward the bandit and flew right up his tailpipe.

Before Cunningham could fully appreciate his victory, hot tracers flashed close past his canopy. Another MiG-17 was closing on his Phantom, so Cunningham put

his fighter into a vicious turn to get away. The stress on the airframe from the turn was so great that wing and flap panels tore off the Phantom. Banked onto his side, Cunningham looked out the top of his canopy and saw his adversary no more than ten feet away. To his amazement, the MiG had turned inside him. With no place else to go, Cunningham dived for some clouds and lit his afterburner, outrunning the MiG while the clouds masked the heat of his exhaust from enemy missiles. He and Driscoll felt fortunate in having escaped.

May 10 was a red-letter day for the two aviators. On that morning, they were part of a force targeted against rail yards in the port city of Haiphong. Their versatile Phantom was armed with bombs for its role as a ground-attack aircraft. Air-to-air weapons consisted of two Sparrows and four Sidewinders.

The first engagement took place just after Cunningham and Driscoll had leveled a brick storage building with their ordnance. They were pulling off the target at high speed when Cunningham's wingman sounded an alarm: "Duke, two MiG-17s at seven o'clock!" Cunningham saw one MiG barreling right at him, tracer fire erupting from its nose cannon. From his days at Top Gun, he remembered that the MiG-17's controls became stiff and unrespon-

Back aboard the U.S. carrier *Constellation* after a day of aerial jousting that would become legendary, Navy pilot Randall Cunningham describes the downing of three MiG-17s on May 10, 1972. He and RIO William Driscoll already had two victories to their credit. The triple kill made them the first U.S. aces of the war.

50

sive at high airspeeds; he shoved his F-4's control stick to one side and turned into the oncoming MiG. The scheme worked; the MiG's pilot couldn't change course quickly enough, and he overshot. Cunningham quickly reversed his turn and found himself about 2,500 feet behind the MiG. Loosing a Sidewinder, he watched it guide right up the tailpipe and explode.

The radio came alive with MiG warnings. To get into good position, both F-4s shot up to 15,000 feet, then rolled over and dived for eight MiG-17s far below them. They were flying in a defensive formation—the Lufbery Circle of World War I, in which each fighter protects the tail of the aircraft ahead of it. Mixed in with the MiGs were three attacking F-4s.

As Cunningham and his wingman approached the circle, an F-4 with two MiGs hot on its tail and one on its wing flashed by. Cunningham pulled out of his dive, rolling out behind the four aircraft that had passed him going the other way. With four planes ahead, it was risky to launch a Sidewinder; it might fly past the MiGs and into the F-4's tailpipe. Cunningham called out over the radio to the Phantom pilot, "Showtime, break right, break right," but the pilot failed to turn. "Showtime, reverse starboard," Cunningham yelled again. "If you don't, you're going to die!"

That message got through, and the F-4 broke right, leaving Cunningham free to shoot his Sidewinder. But there was trouble locking on. First there was a growl, then no growl. The next time the tone sounded, Cunningham fired. The missile ran true and slammed into one of the MiGs, ripping up the entire length of the fuselage. Somehow, the pilot ejected, or was thrown clear of the wreckage.

Cunningham had lost track of his wingman during the melee. "Everywhere I looked," he later remembered, "there were MiGs, and I didn't see any other F-4s around. So I headed east," flying toward the ocean and safety.

As he approached the coast, however, Cunningham spotted a MiG-17 in the distance coming straight at him. "Watch this, Willie," Cunningham told Driscoll, setting up to pass the MiG as closely as possible to make it more difficult for the North Vietnamese pilot to reverse course and latch onto his six. It was another maneuver he had learned and practiced at Top Gun. As the range closed, the MiG opened up with its cannon. Cunningham pulled back on his control stick, heading straight up. He assumed the MiG would head for home.

But this MiG driver did not fit the mold; as he passed Cunningham, he too pulled straight up. The Navy pilot looked back and saw the MiG no more than thirty feet away, canopy-to-canopy with the F-4. Worse, he began to outdistance the MiG even though his airspeed was dangerously low. To avoid flying into his adversary's sights or losing control of his slowing fighter, Cunningham went into a dive. On the way down, the MiG followed, sending a burst of tracer fire uncomfortably close to the F-4. Both fighters tried swinging out wide and then cutting back in a maneuver known as a rolling scissors. This pas de deux continued for several minutes, but neither flier could gain an advantage. Here was no ordinary MiG pilot. "He's going to get lucky one of these times," Cunningham grimly thought.

During the next vertical zoom, Cunningham conjured up one of the oldest tricks in the book. On the way up, he deployed his F-4's speed brakes and went to idle thrust. As he abruptly slowed, the MiG shot out in front of him. Over the top they went once again, but this time Cunningham was in good position behind the North Vietnamese pilot. He had two Sidewinders left, but he hesitated, concerned that they would lock on the heat of the ground rather than the MiG's exhaust.

"I squeezed one off anyway," Cunningham later said. "It came off the rail and went to his airplane. There was just a little flash, and I thought, 'God, it missed him.' I started to fire my last Sidewinder, and suddenly a big flash of flame and black smoke erupted from his airplane. He didn't seem to go out of control, but he flew straight down into the ground and didn't get out."

Once again Cunningham headed for the Constellation, and once again he and his RIO had a close call as a SAM exploded not 400 feet away, severely damaging the F-4's hydraulic systems. As the fluid

An exultant Captain Steve Ritchie climbs from the cockpit of his F-4D Phantom after shooting down a MiG-21 with a Sparrow missile on August 28, 1972. The kill—his fifth MiG-21 in the space of four months— made him the first Air Force pilot ace of the war.

leaked away, control surfaces became less and less responsive, and Cunningham began to lose control. Luckily, he was able to nurse the Phantom out over the Gulf of Tonkin. He and Driscoll ejected and were picked up uninjured by a rescue helicopter.

By the time they arrived, their shipmates on the *Constellation* had arranged a wild victory celebration aboard the ship. Not only had Cunningham and Driscoll made ace this day (both the Navy and the Air Force gave equal credit for kills to pilots and backseaters), but they had bagged their third, fourth, and fifth MiGs all on one mission—a feat that would stand as the only triple kill of the entire war. From classified signal intelligence, Cunningham and Driscoll later learned that they had killed none other than the legendary Colonel Tomb.

Study at Top Gun clearly benefited these two naval aviators, and Navy air-combat statistics from the period following the bombing pause suggest that the training helped others, too. From less than 4 to 1 before the Ault Report, the Navy's kill ratio jumped to 12.5 to 1 afterward. The Air Force kill ratio, however, remained an unimpressive 3 to 1. A partial explanation for the difference lies in the Air Force decision to train pilots against each other flying identical aircraft, a practice later deemphasized.

Moreover, a savvy pilot could become an ace without the benefit of Top Gun experience. Three hours after Cunningham and Driscoll had shot down their fifth MiG, U.S. Air Force F-4s of the 555th Tactical Fighter Squadron out of Udorn, in Thailand, dispatched three MiG-21s. One of them was bagged by Captain Steve Ritchie and his WSO, Captain Chuck DeBellevue, a team that would go on to rack up five kills each. And DeBellevue, flying with another pilot, would get one more kill to become the highest-scoring American ace of the Vietnam War.

By the time the air war over the North ended in January 1973, American fighter forces could draw some valuable conclusions from the experience. It showed that technological superiority could not guarantee victory. Missiles, while attractive in theory, needed much improvement before pilots could rely on them, Cunningham's success with the Sidewinder notwithstanding. And no missile, regardless of its supposed lethality, would again banish the cannon from the weapons suite of America's air-superiority fighters. But most important, the struggle with the NVAF demonstrated that the dogfight was still alive and well. ★

A Primer of Air-Combat Maneuvering

Frequently outnumbered by opponents as fast and well armed as he, a fighter pilot cannot afford to let an opponent approach too near. His chances for downing the enemy and surviving to fight again are best when he attacks from as far away as possible, preferably before he can see his targets—or they can see him—even as specks in the sky. Separated from the enemy by as much as eighty miles, he can lock onto a target with his radar and fire guided missiles from a distance that allows the enemy formation no opportunity to counterattack.

Air combat, however, is rarely so neat. Radar might not detect enemy fighters masked by electronic countermeasures. Moreover, once a pilot makes radar contact, he might not be able to identify the plane as friend or foe. A missile, once fired, may miss. And in skies swarming with hostile aircraft, some will undoubtedly slip through, closing to within visual range where dogfights begin.

For such occasions, a fighter pilot has a repertoire of tactics that he can use to point his fighter toward the enemy and fire his weapons before his opponent succeeds in the same goal. As shown on these and the following pages, the tactics are artful combinations of basic fighter maneuvers—rolls, turns, climbs, and dives with which a skilled pilot in an agile plane may prevail against a single foe. In a contest against even a pair of adversaries, however, a solitary pilot will be fortunate to escape unscathed.

Flying with little horizontal or vertical distance between them, two MiG-29 Fulcrums *(purple)* find themselves caught between an approaching pair of F-16 Fighting Falcons *(blue)* flying a hard left toward a firing position behind it. To thwart this, the Falcon also turns left. Meanwhile, the second F-16 slices down toward the MiGs, forcing them to split up. Slipping past the

1 Caught in lag pursuit, the pilot of an F-16 Falcon *(blue)* doggedly pursues a MiG-29 Fulcrum *(purple)* that is making a defensive turn to the left.

2 To gain the advantage, the Falcon pilot pulls his fighter's nose toward the inside of the turn and dives in afterburner, rolling to position the F-16's nose below and

Swapping Altitude for Airspeed

Supersonic fighters, losing speed with every maneuver, often chase one another at speeds below 300 mph. Under such circumstances, a pilot chasing an adversary around a turn might seem to have the advantage. And he does—if the nose of his aircraft is pointed ahead of the target. By easing his turn a little, the pilot can let the enemy move into perfect position for a kill. Often, however, the nose points behind the target, a situation called lag pursuit. To set up for a shot, the pilot needs to tighten his turn, but doing so may not be possible. Planes locked in combat are often turning as hard as they can. Any attempt to turn tighter could decrease lift, causing the plane to begin sinking. The pursuer would not only lose any opportunity to fire, but he could become the victim of an attack from above. The solution is the maneuver shown here, the low yo-yo.

Cooling a Hot Approach with Gravity

An attacking pilot closing rapidly on a defender can quickly move from a safe position in the quarry's rear hemisphere to a vulnerable area out front. The danger is clear if a fighter simply overtakes a foe, but it is present even in a turning battle where the attacker approaches more from the side. Excess speed could take him across the defender's path, offering an opportunity to reverse his turn and take the offensive. To stay behind the target, an attacker must slow down with a vertical maneuver. If he seems about to overshoot from the side of the defender, he will perform a barrel-roll attack (overleaf). But if he is approaching the quarry more from the rear, he will execute the simpler maneuver shown here, the high yo-yo.

3 Arching high above his opponent, who continues his defensive turn, the F-16 is slowed by gravity to a speed less than the MiG's. More agile at the lower speed, the Falcon turns sharply and slices down toward the Fulcrum, regaining much of the speed lost in the climb. To escape now, the defender would have to pull the nose of his MiG up hard, causing the nose-low F-16 to overshoot.

4 The F-16 completes the high yo-yo maneuver in a dominant position above and close behind the target, the perfect position for a gun kill.

A Spiraling Climb Above and Behind

Before an attacker speeding in toward a target from the side can slow down to avoid overshooting, he must first change course so that he is flying more or less parallel to the quarry. To accomplish this, the pilot on the offensive simply turns to align the fuselage of his aircraft with that of the victim. This part of the maneuver is best accomplished before the target becomes aware of the threat and begins to evade. At this point, the attacker may be as far as a couple of miles to one side of the defender and still moving too fast, but he has positioned himself for a splendid three-dimensional trick to get behind his target: He pulls up, then rolls to the left, tracing part of a spiral through the air above and behind the defender. The spiral bridges the lateral space between the two aircraft as it increases the distance the attacker must fly, helping to prevent him from overshooting. Called a barrel roll, this maneuver is easier to misjudge than the high yo-yo, but it has the advantage of commencing farther away from the enemy plane, where the pilot may not notice the danger until it is too late.

1 Having adjusted his course to fly almost parallel to a MiG-29 *(purple)* ahead of him and off to the left, the pilot of an F-16 is ready to begin a barrel-roll attack.

2 As the MiG begins a defensive turn toward the faster Falcon, the pilot of the F-16 pulls his fighter into the vertical and climbs to slow his approach. As he rises, he begins a barrel roll to the left, moving toward the adversary and keeping him in view.

3 The Falcon, inverted and high above the MiG-29, pulls nose-down and slices toward the target. Assisted by gravity, which shortens the radius of his

4 Leveling his wings at the end of the maneuver, the pilot of the F-16 pulls out of his dive and quickly closes on the bandit's six o'clock. The Falcon, once again

The Grave Consequences of Error

Despite the high-tech equipment and sophisticated weapons fighters carry, no machine can
fully compensate for a pilot's bad timing or poor
judgment. An attacker who starts a high yo-yo or
barrel-roll attack too late, for example, will be
forced to pull his nose excessively high to avoid
overshooting his target. This would give the bandit a chance to dive, gain separation, and perhaps
disengage. Far different results, however, await
the pilot who hopes to mount a hasty gun attack
and rolls down from the top of a high yo-yo or
barrel-roll attack with his nose too low. In a
steep dive, he will be unable to avoid overshooting a bandit that pulls up suddenly. Passing below, he could become entwined in a maneuver
called vertical rolling scissors—a speed-thieving
series of climbs, reversals, and overshoots. The
pilot who tries to break out of this impasse is
likely to be shot down.

1 Preparing for a high-angle gunshot, the
attacker aims the nose of his F-16 *(blue)*
ahead of a MiG-29 *(purple)*, which pulls
its nose upward in defense and climbs

2 Turning the tables high above and canopy-
to-canopy with his one-time assailant, the
pilot of the MiG-29 aims ahead of his opponent and quickly rolls downward. The

3 As both fighters lose altitude and airspeed, the pilot of the Falcon copies
the inverted downward roll of his opponent, who pulls up into the vertical once

A Split-Second Defense against Two Attackers

Even when well executed, the low yo-yo, high yo-yo, and barrel-roll attacks share the flaw of predictability. In a fight against two opponents, concentrating on one bandit for the several seconds needed to perform these maneuvers might allow the other to mount a fatal attack. To stay alive, the outnumbered pilot must leave his adversaries guessing. Rather than execute classic maneuvers, he will fly short, hard turns, follow them with straight-line accelerations, and take shots not after sustained effort but when he can.

Gambits for the End Game

A pilot with an attacker on his tail has only one thought in mind—to prevent him from achieving a position for a successful gun or missile attack. To accomplish this, the defender follows a simple plan that requires intuition and fine timing. First, he turns toward the bandit just as he seems about to shoot. The closer he believes the attacker is to launching a missile or firing his cannon, the harder the defender turns. His hope is to spoil the pursuer's aim and, if possible, force him to overshoot. Depending on who is the better pilot, three outcomes are then possible. If the attacker overshoots, the defender could reverse his turn and take the upper hand in the dogfight. The attacker might instead pull his nose up and begin a high yo-yo or barrel-roll attack. To foil this tactic, the defender would straighten his turn somewhat to increase airspeed, then attempt to escape from the nose-high bandit. The third outcome is less attractive. As the attacker begins firing missiles, the defender will likely have to execute the last-ditch maneuvers shown to defeat it.

3 Seeing that the missile is still tracking, the defender again releases chaff and flares, then pulls his fighter into a vertical roll in a last-ditch attempt to make the missile overshoot. This time, luckily, the missile is successfully decoyed and veers away harmlessly.

4 Inverted at the top of a roll, the Falcon pilot strives to regain sight of his attacker below. Then he dives to rejoin the fight, steeling himself for additional defensive moves as his antagonist maneuvers for the advantage.

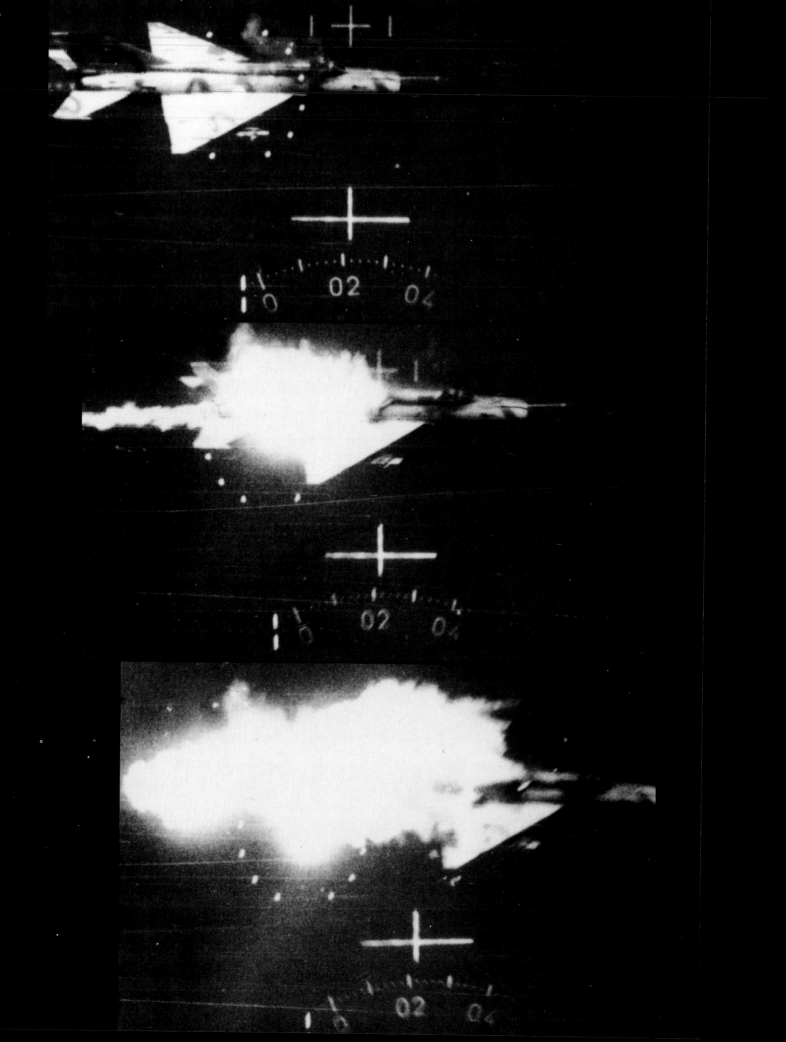

Cauldron in the Middle East

Situated at the crossroads of three continents, its shores lapped by the tides of strategic waterways, its deserts covering a sea of oil, its populations seething with hatreds as old as the hills of Galilee, the Middle East during the second half of the twentieth century has been one of the world's most active battlegrounds. The flash point for most conflicts there has been the tiny state of Israel.

Among the Israeli defense establishment, air superiority is like a religion. Geography makes it so. As constituted in 1948, Israel is only 400 miles long and less than ten miles wide at Tel Aviv. A nation with such dimensions must defend itself beyond its borders or be overrun. Thus, in wartime, Israel has always preferred to take the fight to the enemy—using the Air Force to win absolute control of the skies and then, in concert with the Army, to devastate the foe on the ground. "Israel's best defense," said an early commander of the Israeli Air Force (IAF), "is in the skies over Cairo"—or, he might have added, Baghdad, Damascus, Beirut, or Amman.

In pursuit of that defense, the Israelis have built an air arm that, by every measure except size, equals or exceeds any other such force in the world. Much of that quality is Israel's own doing. But much of it derives from powerful assistance rendered by its allies, primarily the United States, which sought for more than two decades to balance the military assistance provided Arab adversaries by the Soviet Union.

With American arms on one side and Soviet weapons on the other, clashes in the region took on, for both nations, an importance beyond the local political consequences of the fray. For the air battles above the deserts, the superpowers occupied press box seats from which they observed how their combat philosophies, weapons, and tactics fared in the crucible of combat. For the Soviet Union, the results were usually far from satisfactory. In 1982, for example, an astounding Israeli victory in the sky over a little-

69

known valley in Lebanon caused a Soviet self-appraisal and, in the United States, seemed to validate the argument for expensive, high-tech air-combat capabilities. What is more, nearly a decade later, as American forces gathered in Saudi Arabia during yet another Middle East crisis, they would rely heavily on the sophisticated aircraft that had been tested in combat by the IAF.

David and Goliath
over Suez

Early on the morning of October 4, 1969, two Israeli F-4E Phantoms, acquired from the United States only one month earlier, roared off the runway of a Sinai air base and headed east on a reconnaissance mission code-named Operation Hed, Hebrew for "Echo." The big fighters arrowed through a breach that the Israeli Air Force had battered in Egypt's Soviet-supplied surface-to-air missile belt along the Suez Canal. Flying 100 feet above the ground, curving around the derricks and radar masts of cargo ships plying the waterways of the Nile Delta, the Phantoms streaked toward Cairo.

Approaching the great city, the Israeli planes climbed abruptly to 8,500 feet, then rolled into a dive and plummeted toward the Minshat al-Bakkari district, where Egyptian President Gamal Abdel Nasser dwelt in a modest residence. As the pilots pushed their throttles full forward, then outboard and forward again, fuel sprayed into the engine exhausts, lighting off long tails of orange and yellow flame from the afterburners. Bellowing down toward the ground, the Phantoms accelerated past mach 1 and burst through the sound barrier with a pair of earsplitting thunderclaps. Then, as the shock waves reverberated throughout Cairo's teeming, traffic-choked streets, the two Phantoms headed for home. "We dived toward President Nasser's house," one of the Phantom backseaters recalled later, "created the sonic boom, and made a lot of work for Cairo's glaziers that day."

The noisy nuisance raid would have repercussions far beyond Cairo. To Egypt's Nasser, the insulting import of the Israeli incursion was both unmistakable and unendurable. For twenty-eight months, Egypt had been fighting a losing battle to control the skies overhead. When the Egyptian Air Force proved woefully inadequate to the task of keeping the Israelis out, the Egyptian high command attempted to do the job with a dense network of Soviet-supplied SAM batteries and antiaircraft artillery (AAA) arrayed along the east bank of the Suez Canal. But that tactic, too, failed as Israeli fighter-bombers made scrap metal of these defenses. Now, as Operation Hed had made all too evident, the Israeli Air Force had achieved control of the skies: The IAF could fly wherever it wished and do whatever it chose.

Egypt's president would not rest until he had corrected the situation. Less than four months after Operation Hed, on January 22, 1970, Nasser flew to Moscow despite failing health. Throughout four days of secret meetings in the Kremlin, he beseeched his hosts for more planes, more radar, more AAA, and more SAMs. The Soviets were happy to oblige, seizing the opportunity to increase their Mediterranean presence. They ordered twelve SA-2 batteries and several SA-3 batteries, all manned by Soviets, to be placed at the edge of the Suez Canal. These forward defenses would be protected by Soviet fighters overhead. During the next few months, according to London's Institute of Strategic Studies, the "sheer volume of Soviet military support for Egypt was without precedent." Along with the outpouring of air-defense equipment came as many as 20,000 Russian technicians and troops to man it.

Among these reinforcements were ten combat-ready Soviet fighter squadrons—as many as 140 aircraft—transferred from front-line units. The Soviet pilots flew the latest MiG-21. Nicknamed Fishbed J, it had a more powerful engine, better radar, and a more effective fire-control system than earlier versions of the ubiquitous fighter. Most ominously, the new MiG-21s could carry detachable fuel tanks that increased their range enough to attack Israel, if they wished. Upon arrival, the Russians took over six Egyptian airfields and began flying combat air patrols to protect Soviet personnel on the ground.

At first, as if by tacit agreement, both the Israelis and the Soviets refrained from an aerial confrontation. On April 17, for example, upon learning through radio intercepts that Russian pilots were flying cover over an intended target, the IAF recalled a flight of fighter-bombers that was already on its way to the Egyptian interior. Thereafter, the Israelis suspended all deep-penetration attacks, and it seemed as though the Soviet influx had regained a measure of air superiority for Egypt.

However, the Soviets also seemed content to let the Israeli Air

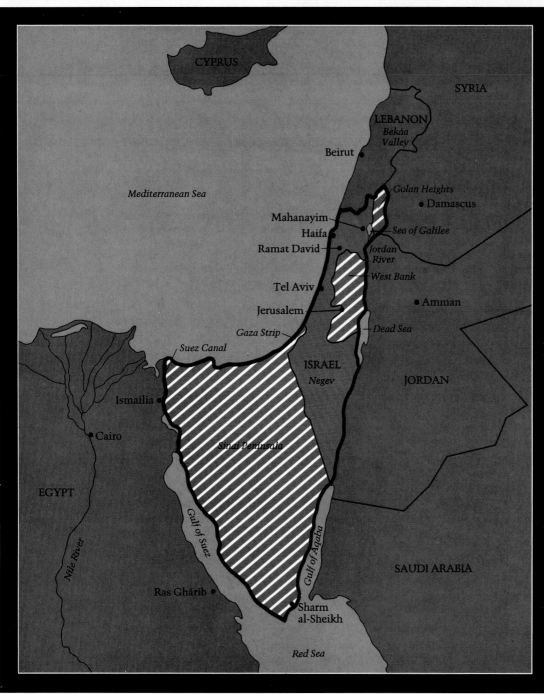

Force rule the skies over a belt extending twenty miles into Egypt from the Suez Canal, an accommodation that was by no means satisfactory to Nasser.

A clash was now inevitable. The catalyst came on July 25, when two Fishbed Js, both piloted by Russians, jumped an Israeli A-4 Skyhawk on a bombing run. Nicknamed Scooter by its pilots, the U.S.-built A-4 was a ground-attack aircraft. Although noted for its maneuverability, it had too little power to take on the MiGs in a dogfight. In this case, the Skyhawk was hopelessly handicapped by the fact that it was in the middle of its bomb run when the Soviets moved in. An infrared-guided AA-2 Atoll missile exploded near the tail assembly, and the Skyhawk almost spun out of control. Only by brilliant flying was the pilot able to keep his plane in the air long enough to reach Israeli lines and crash-land unhurt.

The effect on the IAF was electric. "We had been waiting for something like this to happen for a long time," an Israeli fighter pilot said later. "When they attacked the Skyhawk, we knew that the next step could be for us to take them on in combat—and, frankly, many of us welcomed the opportunity."

Five days later, on the afternoon of July 30, Israeli Air Force commanders decided to bait a trap for the Soviets. To draw out the Russians, Israeli reconnaissance aircraft flew over an Egyptian radar station at Ras Ghārib, on the west side of the Suez Canal. The seemingly helpless recon planes enticed four MiG-21s into the nearby sky. As the recon pilots streaked away, twelve more MiGs took the lure.

High above this activity cruised four Israeli Phantoms and Mirages, with at least a dozen more fighters orbiting not far away. "We didn't lose any time," recalled one of the Phantom pilots. "We had none to lose. We jettisoned our fuel tanks and pounced on them."

Afterward, two Israeli Phantom pilots were permitted to give brief descriptions of the dogfight. Their accounts painted a picture of Soviet air-to-air capabilities stunning in its implications for military forces around the world: As combat pilots, the Russians seemed more like apprentices than masters of their trade.

One of the two Phantom pilots, breaking to his right to go after a MiG that was closing on his flight leader, had been astonished when the Russian, instead of pressing home the attack he had already begun, "left my Number One and started chasing after me. We stuck together for a while, dropping down to about 15,000 feet; at that point he was only about 500 feet from me. I could see the pilot's helmet clearly. By this time I'd realized that the Russian pilot was inexperienced; he didn't know how to handle his aircraft in a combat situation."

Seeming to lose his appetite for the fight, the Russian pointed his nose down in an attempt to disengage. It was a fatal mistake. "All we had to do," the Israeli explained, "was follow him and lock our radar onto him—and fire a missile. There was a tremendous explosion and the Russian aircraft fell apart."

In the second account, another IAF pilot told of Soviet "bait and drag out" tactics. A pair of MiGs came at the Israelis, followed at some distance by a second pair. The hope was that the adversary would fail to see the second pair and turn onto the six o'clock of the first, becoming prey to the trailing MiGs.

The ruse failed. "We let them pass," the Israeli pilot said, "in order not to be sandwiched between the pairs as they had anticipated we would be. They passed one after another as couples in a procession. We waited and got in behind."

"I succeeded in getting my sights on a MiG. He had guts and turned into the fight, but I quickly realized he was inexperienced. He made elementary mistakes. Diving down to 2,000 meters, I cut him off and soon locked on my radar. It was clear that he could not get away." Almost at his leisure, the Israeli closed to a range of 1,000 meters. "We fired a missile. The MiG exploded in a flaming ball."

Within fifteen minutes, the fight was over, and the smoking wreckage of five MiG-21s blackened the desert below. The Israelis had not lost a plane. Eight days later, a dismayed and discouraged Nasser agreed to a cease-fire proposed by the United Nations. And within a month, the Egyptian leader was dead of a heart attack.

Duel in the Sky

After repeated defeats by the Israeli Air Force, Arab pilots were held in generally low esteem by the airmen of other nations. "In an air force such as Syria's," an American fighter pilot once explained, "where you have 600 to 700 jet-qualified pilots, you'll have 15 or 20 exceptionally gifted, knowledgeable aviators and you'll have about 580 hamburgers." On May 12, 1970, during the War of Attrition, Asher Snir, an Israeli deputy squadron commander who would eventually down thirteen enemy aircraft, fought a classic duel with one of the gifted Syrians. Snir and his CO were patrolling over the Golan Heights when they spied a lone Syrian MiG-17 heading northward at low altitude. As Snir later recounted:

> I am a little sad. Amos, who is about 1,000 meters ahead of me, will shoot him down unceremoniously, and it really is not fair. The MiG is all alone, already in front of us, and does not know that he is about to confront a squadron commander and his deputy who, between them, have already put more than one MiG squadron out of business.

No, it is not fair. The MiG-17 is no match for our Mirages. But then this "no match" business is a booby trap; there are fight regimes in the lower- and medium-speed ranges in which the MiG-17 out-turns the Mirage, and whoever is seduced into following a MiG into these territories will get nailed but good.

Amos is closing fast on the MiG, but just as he gets into firing range the MiG breaks sharply up and to the right. He has seen us in time. It was a good maneuver on the MiG's part. An excellent maneuver. Amos pulls up and I enter for a pass and I see the MiG diving, turning sharply and presenting his entire back across my wind-screen. I configure the gunsight, estimate the range. Just as I am about to fire, the MiG twists forcefully and drops even lower. Damn! Screwed up my pass, that man, and I pull out and Amos enters. The man in the MiG takes advantage of the short respite to drop closer to the valley floor and to gather some airspeed, which he will need to continue the fight.

I see the MiG break again just in time, flying practically on the deck, successfully frustrating Amos's pass. I am on my way in. I pull above him, stronger and faster but I'm still unable to get a good shot.

He flies, that man, lower than I have ever seen, knows where to look and when, has excellent vision, and has the concentration and the attention to think clearly, to judge correctly when to do what and not to make any mistakes. I am beginning to understand that we have found a real adversary, and that this battle will be quite different. I could almost visualize the Syrian casting away all the approved rules—rules only applicable to pilots not as good, and situations not as desperate.

This is not the way to fight. One must not fly at such levels of risk that only success separates them from recklessness. But something told me with great certainty that, today and with this man, this was the only way. The entire periphery is etched in my memory as an express tunnel of eight and a half minutes with a series of entries and pull-outs, three volleys which missed, and extremely hard physical effort. I remember him at least once at the bottom of my gunsight, which I could not lower further by even one millimeter because we were already among the tree-tops and he was a couple of agricultural terraces lower than I was.

I remember the Syrian pulling up after me once and both of us climbing out of the valley in cold rage. I remember Amos saying, "Watch out! He's coming after you!" and I, more alive and aware than I had ever been, knowing exactly how much speed the man in the MiG had on his gauge and that he was bluffing.

And so we kept getting further and further north, three madmen joined together till death do us part.

The missile on my wingtip, a Sidewinder-B from America, sends a buzz through my headset from time to time to inform me that it "sees" the MiG. I know that I must not launch at this altitude because the missile will simply dive into the ground directly in front of me if I do not provide it with some room to sink before it has a chance to start homing and climbing.

For a long time I ignore it, until during one of the climb-outs I see that the MiG is about to cross a wide valley at right angles. The man in the MiG does not know this yet, because all he can see from his altitude is the near ridge before the valley, and Amos is almost in firing range already and the Syrian must get busy again and break nicely and correctly among the treetops. So this is my chance.

I do not descend toward the MiG. Instead, I stay at altitude and close the range to 800 meters, the very heart of the missile's flight envelope, and I see the MiG's silver, fishlike silhouette evading Amos's Mirage once again and twisting northward, homeward. The MiG is skimming the rocks, following a narrowing valley that is turning into a dry river bed, climbing within its walls to the top of the ridge.

Now!

With the sight on the distant tailpipe, I hear the missile's battle cry at once. Before the Syrian has a chance to notice that the ground is about to fall away from under him, I launch. A sharp "whoosh!" and the missile is on its way.

The missile crossed the ridge successfully, still sinking, two seconds later, registering a new world record for low-altitude flight by a missile. It continued to sink some more in the valley before it started climbing, homing steadily on the MiG.

Something caused the Syrian to do the very last thing in his life. Perhaps he saw the distant portion of the missile's smoke trail; perhaps he grew suspicious. When the missile was about fifty meters behind him, the man began a break to the right, still within the valley. It was too close and it was too late.

The last second of the brave and talented man's life is still etched in my memory: the missile with its thin smoke plume hiding beneath the wing; the large orange flash which was almost certainly a direct hit; the right wing breaking at the root; the fast, uncontrolled roll toward the missing wing; the grotesque spin of the stubby fuselage. Then came the unavoidable crash of the broken MiG into the distant, steep wall of the valley and the ugly black mushroom that sprouted from the green terrain.

The man in the MiG. A famous hero or an unknown just starting to blossom, he was deserving of one more thing, and to this day I hope that it was granted to him. I hope he died instantly when the missile hit and did not live that last second and never, never knew that he lost the battle.

Reckoning on the Day of Atonement

On October 6, 1973—the Jewish holiday Yom Kippur—Egypt's President Anwar Sadat, successor to Gamal Abdel Nasser, launched 240 fighters and fighter-bombers in a massive surprise attack against Israeli air bases in the Sinai. Simultaneously, 100 Syrian aircraft struck Israeli positions on the Golan Heights. The aerial assault signaled the start of the fifth major war in less than twenty-five years between Israel and its Arab neighbors, and for the next eighteen days, as Israel's ground forces struggled desperately to roll back its enemies' 4,800 tanks and 500,000 soldiers, the Air Force fought its own fierce battle for control of the skies. The combat was the bloodiest in the forty-year history of the IAF. That Israel emerged triumphant was due to the valor and skills of its aircrews.

To be sure, Israel's F-4 Phantoms and French-built Mirage IIIs were superior to the Arabs' Soviet-supplied MiG-21s and MiG-17s. But machinery was not the critical factor. "Training," a top Israeli officer once said, "is of greater importance and significance than the means of warfare, the weapons systems, and the technology." The world's air forces have always been manned by well-motivated volunteers, certainly among the aircrews. But the IAF sets itself apart by the extraordinary caliber of its recruits and the intensity of its training. So many young men—mostly eighteen-year-olds reared on tales of past IAF glories—clamor to join up that, as one officer put it, "we have the privilege of choosing the best, about one percent, of all high school graduates nationwide." After extensive psychological and physical tests, about 2,000 applicants each year are accepted for the Air Force, and of those, perhaps 300 are chosen for pilot training.

In the first stages of a two-year course near the ancient town of Beersheba, the pilot candidates are tested for leadership, flexibility, and the initiative to improvise—all qualities highly prized by the Israeli Air Force—in grueling field exercises that include commando, paratrooper, and desert survival training. Between classroom sessions in a rigorous ground-school schedule, would-be Israeli pilots learn to fly in small training jets, beginning with basic maneuvers and progressing, for potential fighter pilots, to gunnery and aerobatics. Those who demonstrate anything less than superb aptitude—at least a third of every class—are ruthlessly washed out. Finally, after 250 hours of flight time (approximately 25 percent more than U.S. Air Force practice), the 200 or so survivors win their cherished wings. Of that elite group, only forty are tapped to fly fighters in operational squadrons. There training continues apace, with constant practice in aerial marksmanship and dogfighting, sometimes against captured MiGs. "We fly and fight six days a week, fifty-two weeks a year," says a senior IAF pilot. Yet no matter how experienced a pilot might be or how distinguished a record he might earn, he would be grounded if his skills betrayed any slight sign of diminishing.

The prowess of Israel's fighter pilots was well known to neighboring Arab nations. In preparing for the Yom Kippur War, for example, Egypt's Sadat had seen to it that training for Egyptian pilots

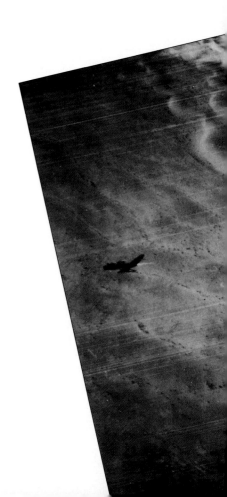

Afterburner blazing, an Egyptian MiG-17 *(left, below)* tries to escape an Israeli F-4 Phantom during a dogfight over the Sinai in the 1973 Yom Kippur War. Moments after his wingman snapped this photo, the Israeli pilot downed the MiG with a burst from his 20-mm Vulcan cannon.

was greatly intensified. Even so, his aviators averaged only about forty hours of flying time per month—less than half the Israeli norm. Moreover, there was no great rush by young Egyptians—or Syrians, for that matter—to become part of an air force that had been repeatedly humiliated by the IAF. Indeed, on that fateful Day of Atonement in 1973, about 150 of Egypt's 768 planes were idle for lack of pilots. (The Israelis, by contrast, had three highly qualified pilots for every aircraft.) Moreover, Arab pilots were trained by Soviet instructors who treated them as inferiors and drilled them in blind adherence to rigid doctrine. "They genuinely hate their Russian advisers," said an American pilot familiar with the Middle East. "The Russian technique of training is, 'You will do it this way.' And, of course, the Arabs think differently."

Sadat's intention on October 6 was to turn the tables on Israel, which had suprised Egypt's air force on the ground in the Six-Day War of 1967. In one of the first attacks, at two o'clock in the afternoon on October 6, sixteen Egyptian MiG-17s swept in to bomb the Israeli air base at Sharm al-Sheikh in the southern Sinai while a dozen MiG-21s flew top cover. Seconds before the MiGs arrived, a pair of F-4 Phantoms had scrambled to the defense. Neither Israeli crew had seen combat before, and they suffered their share of jitters. Yet within a few minutes, they had shot down seven of the attackers with missiles and cannon fire. A captain identified only as N got four MiGs, while his wingman splashed three, including one MiG-17 frantically skimming the Red Sea so low that it spanked the water several times. As the huge F-4 closed in for the kill, its own exhaust raised great twin rooster tails of spray from the sea. In the days that followed, the IAF threw itself into an all-out air-to-ground attack on the enemy, and suffered grievously—not from Egyptian and Syrian interceptors, but from an unexpectedly sophisticated air defense system of surface-to-air missiles and antiaircraft artillery. Between them, the Egyptians and Syrians had established no fewer than 220 SAM and 2,500 AAA sites that included 221 of the deadly ZSU-23-4s, four-barrel, radar-aimed 23-mm weapons that were capable of spewing out 4,000 high-explosive rounds per minute.

Israeli intelligence had discounted these developments; since 1967, a growing belief in Israeli invincibility had led to ever-rosier military-intelligence reports that played down the capabilities of the nation's enemies. Half of all IAF planes lost in the eighteen days of warfare would be downed by SAMs and another 40 percent would be hit by antiaircraft artillery.

But the Israeli Air Force is noted for its initiative and flexibility. Within the first week of the war, mechanics installed on the Phantoms radar-defeating electronic countermeasures (ECM) equipment rushed from the United States, and the pilots devised low-level, pop-up bombing tactics with which the IAF began to punch holes in the air defense umbrella. Through the gaps poured dozens of fighter-bombers to attack vulnerable airfields and rear areas. The Arabs had little choice but to tackle Israeli fighters and fighter-bombers in the sky and diverted 80 to 90 percent of their sorties from attack to defense.

The strategy failed. By October 16, the Egyptians had lost more than 170 aircraft in air-to-air combat, while only five Israelis had fallen to Anwar Sadat's airmen. The Syrians fared better. In three days, from October 10 to October 12, the Syrian Air Force saw sixty-eight of its aircraft go down versus only fifteen for the Israelis. However, virtually all of the Arab losses resulted from swirling aerial battles, while Israeli planes fell almost exclusively to SAMs and the murderous ZSU-23s.

Arab airmen fought courageously, but they were simply outclassed by their Israeli opponents. During a mission over the Nile Delta on October 14, for example, one low-flying Israeli pilot was jumped by a MiG-21 that "made a quarter pass at my aircraft with

An Egyptian pilot successfully bails out of his downed MiG and parachutes to the ground *(left)*, only to be met there by members of the Israeli Defense Forces *(below)*. For him, the war is over. However, the duel over the desert during the Yom Kippur War was a protracted one, with the IAF achieving no more than localized air superiority.

his gun, but he didn't lead me enough and missed." The Israeli pilot looked out and saw another MiG firing at his wingman from a distance of 400 yards. "A great flame was leaping out of his cannon," he recalled. "I yelled for the wingman to break right, and he did. I cleaned up my plane by dumping my bombs and fuel." Lining up behind the MiG that was shooting at his wingman, the pilot launched a Sidewinder missile. Fearful that the missile would be attracted by heat from his wingman's engines, the pilot immediately ordered the wingman to break away. But it was a narrow thing. "The Sidewinder guided to the right, I thought it was going for my wingman," the pilot recalled. "But it came back and hit the MiG, blowing him up."

With his bombs gone and his missiles expended, the Israeli streaked out over the Mediterranean for home. "Now I was very low on fuel," he said later, "and I started to climb to save fuel. All of a sudden a missile flashed by. I looked back and saw a MiG-21. I went up and the MiG climbed with me, and he came within 100 meters. I could see him clearly—he was wearing a leather helmet.

"I thought to myself, so this is how it will end—no missiles, almost no fuel, over the cold water, and this guy seems good. Up we went. But I had one trick left. At 250 knots I engaged the afterburners and nosed over. He tried to follow me down, but evidently lost control because he started spinning and flew right into the water with a big splash."

The final tallies on October 24, when the combatants accepted a U.N.-sponsored cease-fire, are a matter of conjecture. Few take seriously the Arab claim to have downed 303 Israeli aircraft, and the Israeli claim to 550 Arab planes appears to be exaggerated as well. The best estimate is that, at the end of the Yom Kippur War, the Egyptians and Syrians together were poorer by some 447 aircraft, no fewer than 277 of them victims of Israeli pilots. For its part, the IAF is thought to have lost a total of 109 planes, of which only eleven were shot down in air-to-air fighting. Among that number was an F-4 downed by an Egyptian helicopter firing rockets as the Phantom attempted to fly beneath it.

In the air, at least, the two-and-a-half-week war was no contest. The Israeli kill ratio of 22 to 1 represented a feat of arms unprecedented in modern air warfare. And yet before the decade had passed, the IAF would vastly surpass even that record in an astonishing aerial melee above a little-known valley in Lebanon.

A New Generation of Fighters

With a low whistle of twin turbofan engines, four of the big new fighters came winging in over the Mediterranean from the west and peeled off into their landing break. Moments later, tires chirped against the runway at an airfield near Ramat David. It was Friday, December 10, 1976, and the first of fifty-one state-of-the-art F-15 Eagles purchased from the United States had arrived in Israel.

The Eagles brought a collective sigh of relief from Israeli Air Force commanders. After almost a decade of combat, the F-4 Phantom was becoming obsolescent. Various upgrades would extend its life into the twenty-first century, but there was a clear need for a new aircraft. That need had seemed urgent in the late 1960s, when the Soviet Union unveiled the MiG-23 Flogger. Boasting swing wings and mach 2.3 (1,520 mph) speed, it would later be supplied to Syria. As it turned out, the Flogger—and an even faster jet called the MiG-25 Foxbat—were vastly overrated. But in the meantime, the American response was the McDonnell Douglas F-15 Eagle. First produced in 1972, the fighter was awesome in every respect, from its ability to go supersonic in a vertical climb to its superior agility and unequaled radar and weapons systems.

At a cost of $16 million a copy, the Eagle was expensive even in U.S. terms. But as might be expected from a country whose very existence depended on cutting-edge aerial technology, Israel became the first overseas customer for the F-15—and the first to blood the fighter in combat. On June 27, 1979, a flight of F-15s covering a fighter-bomber strike against terrorists in southern Lebanon took on almost a dozen Syrian MiG-21s that rose to challenge. Five of the MiGs were shot down within forty-five seconds, and one victorious young Israeli pilot exulted: "The things you can do with the Eagle are simply amazing. With other aircraft, the moment comes when you have to plead with the engine for more power, more speed. Here, your only limitation is your own endurance." A few months later, four more Syrian fighters—MiG-23s this time—were destroyed without damage to the Eagles. In the months that followed, another dozen MiGs were shot down in patrol actions without the loss of a single Eagle.

By then, an able young cousin to the Eagle also had joined the IAF.

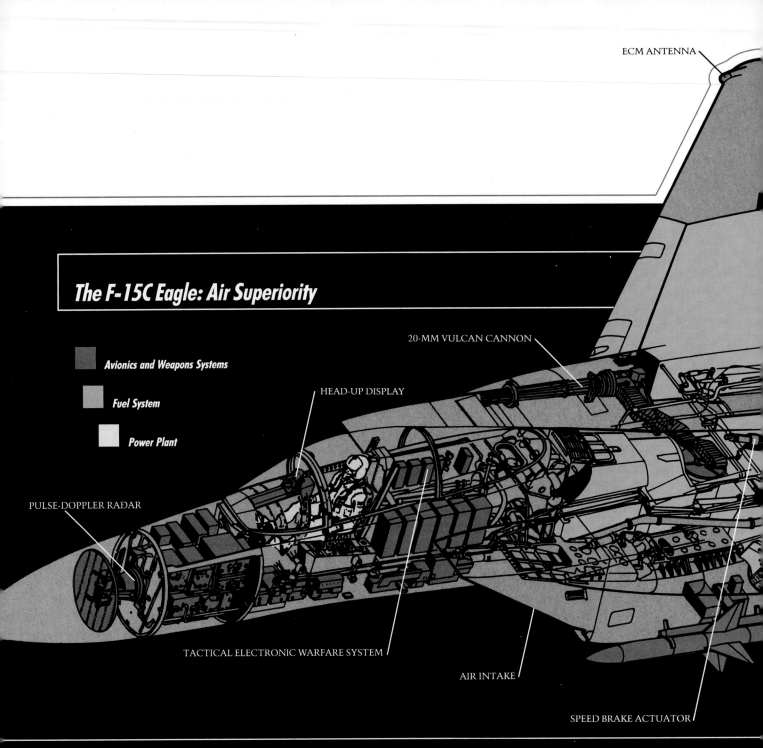

The F-15C Eagle: Air Superiority

■ **Avionics and Weapons Systems**

■ **Fuel System**

□ **Power Plant**

ECM ANTENNA

20-MM VULCAN CANNON

HEAD-UP DISPLAY

PULSE-DOPPLER RADAR

TACTICAL ELECTRONIC WARFARE SYSTEM

AIR INTAKE

SPEED BRAKE ACTUATOR

By all odds the best air-combat fighter of the mid-1970s and 1980s, the McDonnell Douglas F-15 Eagle is a quantum leap ahead of the Vietnam-era F-4 Phantom. And even with the advent of two capable new Soviet fighters, the MiG-29 Fulcrum and Su-27 Flanker, the Eagle remains the world standard.

In its C model, the single-seat Eagle is powered by twin Pratt & Whitney F100 turbofans that generate almost 48,000 pounds of thrust, enough to give it a thrust-to-weight ratio of 1.4 to 1 for superior ac-

celeration and a dash speed of mach 2.5 (1,650 mph). The Eagle can fly and fight at 65,000 feet, and has long legs for a fighter: It can carry more than 13,000 pounds of fuel in tanks in the wings and fuselage, and low-drag conformal cellular packs that attach to the air intakes add another 10,000 pounds; together they give the F-15 a ferry range of 3,450 miles without refueling—or five hours of combat air patrol.

At the heart of the F-15's avionics are a tactical electronic warfare system, which

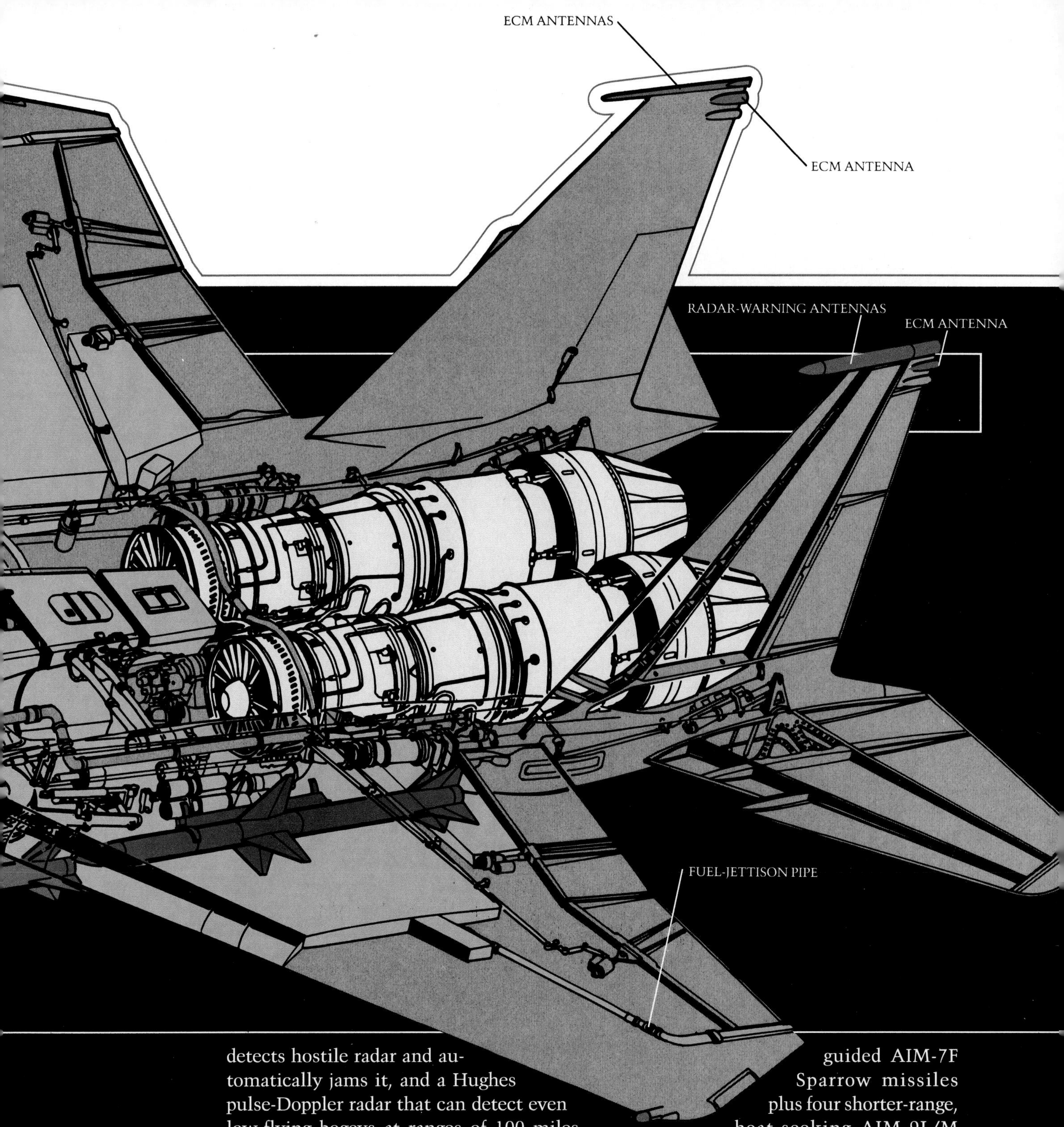

ECM ANTENNAS

ECM ANTENNA

RADAR-WARNING ANTENNAS

ECM ANTENNA

FUEL-JETTISON PIPE

detects hostile radar and automatically jams it, and a Hughes
pulse-Doppler radar that can detect even
low-flying bogeys at ranges of 100 miles.
Target information—and other flight and
weapons data—is fed to a central computer,
which flashes it on a head-up display at the
front of the bubble canopy, where the pilot
can read it without looking down at the instrument panel. He can then select from a
formidable array of weapons: The F-15 nor-

guided AIM-7F
Sparrow missiles
plus four shorter-range,
heat-seeking AIM-9L/M
Sidewinders mounted under the wings.
Like all U.S. fighters, the Eagle carries a cannon for close-in fighting. The weapon is the
M61 Vulcan, and it is a fiery forge indeed,
with six spinning barrels spitting out 6,000
high-explosive 20-mm shells per minute.
Even a one-second burst can reduce an en-

The Israeli Air Force's unparalleled success in battle stems from many factors: state-of-the-art equipment, brilliant tactics, superbly trained and supremely motivated aircrews. And there is something else: The IAF has always enjoyed what may well be the world's most effective ground support.

Like everyone else in the Air Force, mechanics and technicians are volunteers chosen from thousands of applicants. The training is rigorous, the washout rate high, and the squadron drill incessant, but in war, the IAF's ground crews are unequaled. One analyst has estimated that because of them, the IAF was able to fly an astonishing 10,500 sorties out of a theoretical limit of 11,000 from its 480 warplanes during the Yom Kippur War. Moreover, of 236 aircraft damaged in combat, no fewer than 215 were back in service within a week.

In the Bekáa Valley campaign of 1982, every one of Israel's seventy-two F-16 Falcons was ready for combat every morning. When an Israeli fighter returned from a sortie, it often was refueled and rearmed within ten minutes, faster than the pilot could be briefed for his new mission. As one IAF ground crewman puts it: "We get paid for our hard work when the pilot is safely home—and sometimes we get the bonus of a downed MiG in the video camera."

Hustling across the tarmac, two Israeli ground-crew members (above) run out an external fuel tank and ordnance to a waiting Kfir C2 jet fighter during the 1982 Lebanon war.

In 1975, the Americans had developed a much less expensive lightweight fighter, the General Dynamics F-16 Falcon. With only one engine, the Falcon gave up to the Eagle about 300 mph in speed, some radar and standoff missile capability—and a lot of weight. The result was a fabulously maneuverable aircraft that, at a price of $6.76 million each, was one of the great military bargains of all time. What was more, while the Eagle was designed primarily for air superiority, the Falcon was built to perform equally well as a fighter-bomber. Israel ordered seventy-five of them. They had scarcely entered the inventory when, in June of 1981, they flew 1,200 miles round trip to destroy with surgical precision an Iraqi nuclear reactor that Israel suspected would soon be producing ingredients for atomic weapons.

These then would be the players—F-15s and F-16s on the Israeli side, MiG-21s and MiG-23s in the Syrian ranks—the following year in one of history's great dramas of air combat. Before it was over, the Israeli Air Force would not only demonstrate indisputable superiority in men and machines but would also orchestrate a phenomenal display of electronic C3I—command, control, communications, and intelligence—that would change the face of war in the air.

The scene was set in July 1981 with the failure of a week-old cease-fire between Israel and the Lebanon-based Palestine Liberation Organization. After agreeing to a truce, each side began to interpret the terms to its own advantage. Israel resumed overflights of Lebanon and the strafing of Palestinian camps from which the PLO was staging terrorist raids and lobbing Katyusha rockets, artillery rounds, and tank shells into northern Israel.

By the spring of 1982, the Israelis had become determined to reestablish a protective buffer zone along their northern frontier, which had been policed by anti-PLO Lebanese Christian forces. Israeli troops and tanks swept into Lebanon on June 6 in Operation Peace for Galilee, a campaign that was intended to rid the area of PLO troops. Syria intervened with its ground forces, protected by surface-to-air missiles situated in the Bekáa Valley, a narrow, seventy-five-mile-long plain between 6,500-foot mountain ranges east of Beirut.

Israel had known for some months about the missile emplacements, mostly deadly SA-6s of Yom Kippur fame, along with some SA-2s and SA-3s. And while diplomatic initiatives sought and failed to end the threat against Israel from southern Lebanon, the IAF

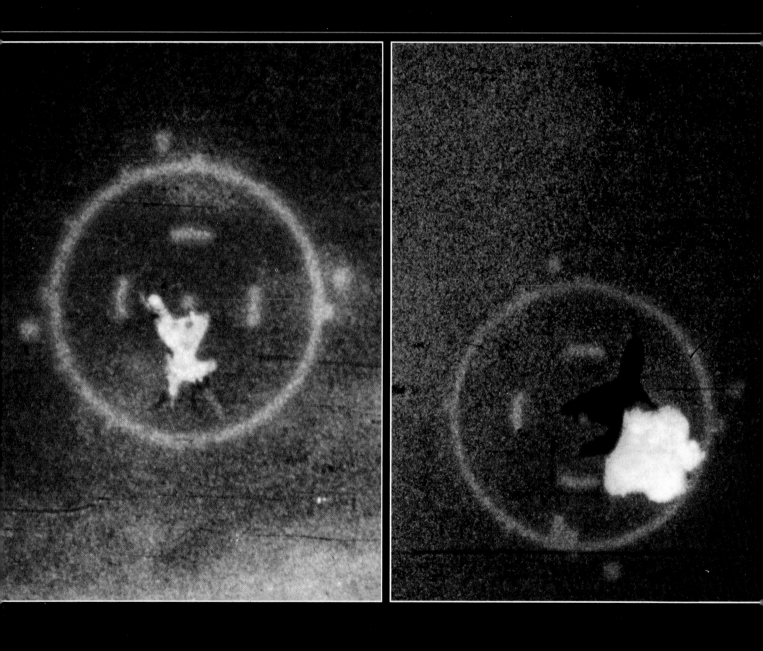

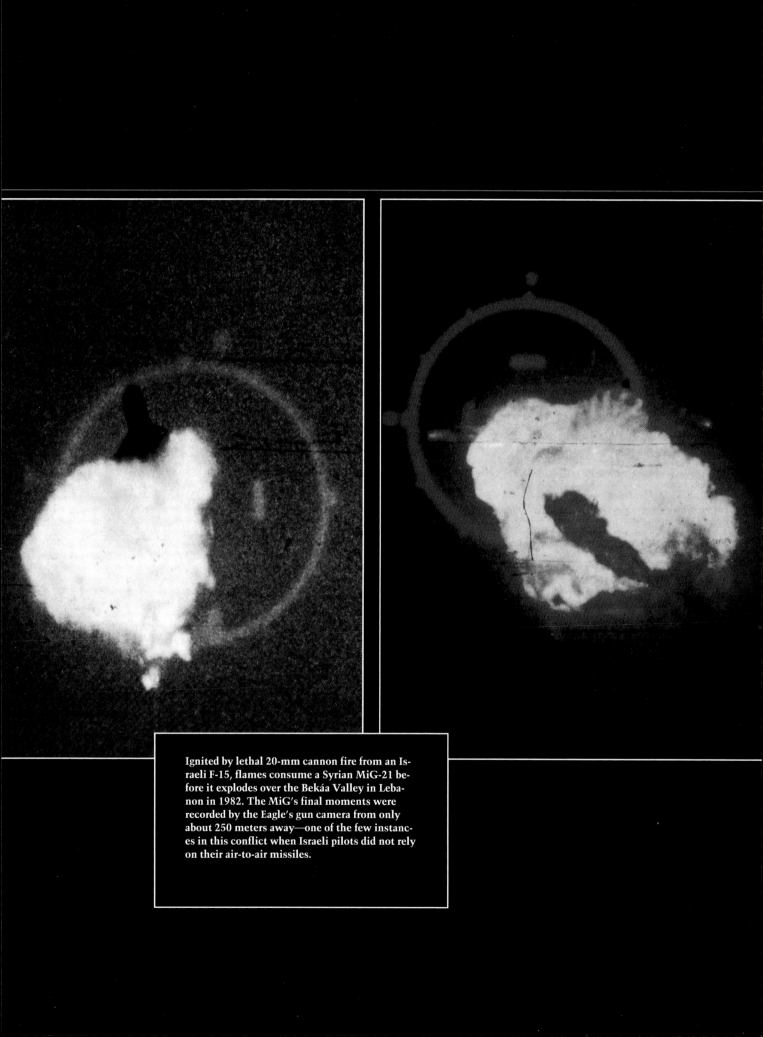

Ignited by lethal 20-mm cannon fire from an Israeli F-15, flames consume a Syrian MiG-21 before it explodes over the Bekáa Valley in Lebanon in 1982. The MiG's final moments were recorded by the Eagle's gun camera from only about 250 meters away—one of the few instances in this conflict when Israeli pilots did not rely on their air-to-air missiles.

made plans to knock out the SAM sites in the Bekáa Valley should the need arise—as it did with the launching of Peace for Galilee.

On the morning of June 9, as many as seventy intelligence-gathering Scout and Mastiff remotely piloted vehicles (RPVs) were catapulted from trucks and sent like a pack of beagles, sensors sniffing, into the Bekáa Valley. Designed and built in Israel, the little (eleven feet long, 135 pounds dry weight) drones appeared as if they might have been glued together by an ambitious hobbyist. But they bore gyroscopically stabilized TV cameras with zoom lenses that transmitted live pictures of enemy activity to mobile ground control centers for viewing on large screens by Israeli commanders. When the Scouts and Mastiffs finished their morning's work, they had pinpointed nineteen missile batteries, most of them SA-6s, that the Syrians had installed in the Bekáa Valley.

Next, an odd-looking, twin-turboprop aircraft rumbled off an Israeli airfield. The plane bore on its back a horizontally rotating, saucer-shaped shell twenty-four feet in diameter called a rotodome. Inside the dome was the antenna of a powerful radar system. As the rotodome turned lazily, the aircraft headed west toward the Mediterranean and began cruising slowly up and down the Levantine coast, sixty miles offshore.

This was one of four Grumman E-2C Hawkeye Airborne Early Warning (AEW) aircraft developed for U.S. Navy carrier battle groups and purchased by Israel for airborne command and control. In the Hawkeye's cramped, electronics-packed fuselage, waves of nausea swept over one of the three systems operators. He suffered from a condition fairly common among Hawkeye crews; it was caused by the unusually flat turns required to prevent the massive radar antenna from banging against the inside of the rotodome. Fighting off his airsickness, the crewman concentrated on one of the circular screens that would give him and another operator a god's-eye view of more than three million cubic miles of air space and detect fighter planes up to 250 miles away. Behind them, the Hawkeye's mission commander fine-tuned the radio links that could enable him to direct fighter operations.

Only the western edge of the valley, masked by mountains, would escape the Hawkeye's electronic gaze. To cover those sectors, F-15 Eagles serving as mini-AEWs would provide surveillance with look-down radar that could pick aircraft out of the ground clutter at distances of more than seventy miles (pages 98-105).

As the Hawkeye and Eagles approached their surveillance stations, F-4E Phantoms were rolled out of concrete shelters at Israel's Haifa, Mahanayim, and Ramat air bases. The venerable Phantoms were now used almost exclusively in a ground-attack role, and for that purpose the twenty-six F-4Es in the first wave had been armed with the latest American SAM-site eradicators. For visual attack, there were TV-guided AGM-65 Maverick missiles with a range of fifteen miles. Some of the Phantoms carried antiradar missiles, either Vietnam-vintage AGM-45 Shrikes intended to home on radar signals transmitted by SAM batteries as they tracked potential targets or, for the first time in battle, AGM-78 Standard Arms. This missile was designed to eliminate a shortcoming of the Shrike, which lost its bearings if the radar it had targeted was turned off by the missile crew on the ground. The Standard Arm has an inertial guidance system that keeps it going in the direction from which it has last heard a signal. The antiradar F-4s can, in the words of one pilot, "ride missiles on a beam right down the bastards' throats."

With a final thumbs-up from the ground crews, the Phantoms blasted off the runways, hugged the deck as they sped north toward the Bekáa Valley, and began to orbit behind hills. They were awaiting the final notes of the prelude that would open the show.

Although the doughty little Scouts and Mastiffs had already pinpointed the Syrian SAMs, the powerful search radars that told the SAM sites where to look for targets had yet to be precisely located. And so, across the sky of the Bekáa Valley came another parade of drones, this time air-launched Samsons and truck-launched Delilahs carrying reflectors that made them appear on Syrian radar screens as full-sized warplanes. One after another, the Syrian radars blinked on and, as their operators sought to track the "attacking" aircraft, revealed their own whereabouts as clearly as if they were lighthouse beacons.

That was all the F-4s needed. At 2:00 p.m.—exactly on schedule—they streaked low out of their staging area behind the hills into the Bekáa Valley, then popped up to 7,000 feet and unleashed their missiles. Seconds later, a Shrike detonated above a radar antenna, flailing the control van with debris from the explosion. A Maverick pulverized another radar and its crew. Within ten minutes, most of the SAM batteries had been blinded and lay vulnerable to a second wave of Israeli strikers.

On Syrian airfields to the east, some of them less than two min-

Struck by a Soviet-made Syrian SA-8 surface-to-air missile, an Israeli F-4 comes to a blazing end in Lebanon. Remarkably, one of the Phantom's two crew members survived —and was taken prisoner by Syrian troops.

utes' flying time from the Bekáa Valley, Syrian MiGs had scrambled in the opening moments of the Israeli onslaught. During the fateful minutes now at hand, Syrian commanders and their Soviet advisers would commit at least sixty aircraft—more than 10 percent of the Syrian fighter force—to the Bekáa Valley in a foredoomed attempt to protect the SAM sites.

Stationed in the sky above at least three Syrian airfields, Scout RPVs transmitted the sight of MiGs taxiing for takeoff. Recalled an Israeli officer: "One of the most exciting television pictures I have ever seen was when four aircraft were taking off from a base in Syria, trying to find the Scout while we were watching them through its gimbaled camera. They never found it."

As soon as the MiGs were airborne, they triggered a sequence of actions aboard the offshore Hawkeye. Radar data pouring into the E-2C was instantly analyzed by an on-board computer that flashed aircraft symbols representing hostiles and friendlies onto console screens; displayed statistics about the speed, altitude, and range of bogeys; and calculated the geometry to carry out an intercept. Upon receiving this information from the system operators, the Hawkeye's mission commander selected a fighter unit to do the job and, in calm, clipped words, gave them their orders.

As many as ninety Israeli fighters were waiting and ready, flying carefully layered combat air patrols just west of the Bekáa Valley. F-15 Eagles cruised at 30,000 feet, positioned to take advantage of the look-down capability of their sophisticated radars. At the lower altitudes flew F-16 Falcons and Israeli-built Kfirs, whose less capable radars worked best with targets silhouetted against the sky. At a safe remove from the battle orbited a quartet of Boeing 707s, their passenger seats replaced by racks of electronic black boxes that selectively bombarded enemy radio frequencies. The disruptive power of these planes was such that four years before the Bekáa Valley confrontation now shaping up, an American pilot had felt its electronic effects while training Jordanians 120 miles from the scene of a border clash between Israeli and Syrian fighters. "I couldn't even talk to my wingman," he recalled. "Com-jamming was quite severe."

To secure their own communications from Syrian electronic countermeasures, Israeli radios were equipped with a newly developed electronic counter-countermeasures device that skipped so rapidly across a broad range of radio frequencies that enemy jamming units could not follow.

As the Syrian pilots blasted into the valley, they were met by an electronic storm from the 707s that completely disrupted their communications. Because of their almost total reliance on ground controllers to direct them, the Syrians were particularly vulnerable to jamming. Within seconds, Syrian formations began to flounder— and the Israeli fighters came screaming in.

The Israelis had every advantage. The Arab pilots were outnumbered. Their stripped-down Soviet export versions of the MiG-21 and MiG-23 were badly outmatched in performance by the Israeli Eagles and Falcons. The Soviet airborne radars were distinctly inferior to those in the Israeli fighters. And the Soviet AA-2 Atoll and AA-8 Aphid infrared-guided missiles, effective only when fired from within a narrow cone extending from an enemy's tail, could not equal the Israelis' U.S.-supplied radar-guided Sparrows or the advanced Sidewinders, both of which could be fired from any angle. For their part, the Israelis had developed their own all-aspect heat seeker, the Python III, with a bigger warhead than the Sidewinder's and greater turning ability.

As if all that were not enough, the Syrians used standard Soviet tactics, flying in massed groups designed to shatter enemy formations by sheer weight of numbers and then pick off individual aircraft. Now, however, bereft of communications with their ground controllers, the MiGs began milling around in confusion. "I watched a group of Syrian fighter planes fly figure-eights," a Western military observer recalled. "They just flew around and obviously had no idea what to do next."

The result was a turkey shoot. By the time the MiGs tried to break away, the Eagles and Falcons had already locked onto them and were readying their missiles.

One Israeli major flying an F-16 had just taken out a missile battery when he saw a pair of MiGs. He pointed the nose of his plane at the tail of one of them. "The eye of the missile is on the tail of the airplane—the tone is in my ear," the major later wrote of the encounter. "I release my missile seeker. It informs me through the computer that it's locked onto the MiG's engine."

The major fired one missile. "Five seconds pass—they seem an eternity until the missile explodes with a small plume of smoke. Contact. The MiG simply stands still in the air. Another second and his right wing is suddenly torn from place; the aircraft spins and catches fire. A pull on the stick in order to go over him. I see the pilot jump and his parachute opens. Whoever decided to buy the F-16 had this moment in mind."

From above, the covering F-15s were having their own field day. An Israeli Eagle squadron leader later recounted how he and his wingman went after a pair of Syrian MiG-23s. "Quickly we split up the prey between us," he said. "I took the left one, my No. 2 took the right. Launching a missile, I saw the MiG-23 directly hit, with the pilot ejecting immediately, his red-and-white parachute quickly opening below."

Eagle number two also nailed a MiG, and the fight continued. "Only a few seconds later, two more Syrians were detected," continued the pilot. This time the bandits were MiG-21s, which "acted as if they did not see us at all—they flew on totally ignoring us. Again, we shared the prey." Approaching from a position outside the enemy's radar sweep, the squadron leader closed "to effective gun range. A first burst missed the target, the second burst hit home but the MiG was only slightly hit. He reared up and attempted to evade, making speed towards Syria."

"Chasing after him, I fired a third gun burst," the Israeli recounted. This time he hit the Syrian hard. "Smoke started to come out, followed by a shattering explosion."

This pilot's experience was typical in all but one respect. By downing a MiG with his cannon instead of a missile, he had done something that had become increasingly rare with improvements in air-to-air missiles. During the War of Attrition in the late 1960s and early 1970s, when the IAF was armed with unreliable Vietnam-era missiles, fighters bearing the Star of David had scored 70 percent of their victories with cannon fire. Now, over the Bekáa Valley, missiles were accounting for 93 percent of Israel's kills. According to an Israeli flier who shot down six MiGs during the Peace for Galilee operation, most of his kills came at an altitude of about 5,000 feet from an average distance of 1,400 yards—point-blank range for a Sidewinder or a Python. Of the victories attributed to gunfire, there were indications that at least some Israeli pilots used their cannon more for the sport of it than out of necessity.

The squadron leader's battle with the MiG-21 was also one of the few real dogfights on that June afternoon. An overwhelming majority of the Syrian victims were shot down by Eagles and Falcons vectored by the Hawkeye and by the F-15s playing a battle-management role into positions abeam of the MiGs. Streaking in from the side, Israeli pilots could comfortably launch their missiles without appearing on the Syrian fighters' radar.

By 2:30 p.m., when a second wave of Israeli strike aircraft departed from the Bekáa Valley after plastering enemy missile sites with television-guided Mavericks and cluster bombs, the surviving MiGs had fled. They left behind them the plumes of smoke, gently wafted by an afternoon breeze, that rose from the wrecks of twenty-two Syrian fighters and one helicopter. As dusk fell—and after a third and fourth wave of bombers had roared in—seventeen of the nineteen Syrian SAM batteries had been destroyed. The following morning, as IAF attack planes returned to the valley for the two remaining SAM sites and an Israeli ground force moved into the lower Bekáa Valley, Syrian fighters again swarmed from their bases—and again the Eagles and Falcons were waiting. This time, twenty-five MiGs and three helicopters were sent spinning out of the sky. On the morning of June 11, the Syrians attempted once more to seize control of the air space over the Bekáa Valley—at a cost of eighteen MiGs.

By the end of July, when the fighting in Lebanon finally wound down, Syria had lost eighty-five MiGs, 19 percent of its combat planes. Of those, forty had been shot down by Eagles and forty-four by Falcons; one MiG fell to a Phantom that found itself in an air-to-air fight after making its bomb run. Incredibly, not one of Israel's fighters had been lost in air combat, though a number had been damaged, including an F-15 that somehow made it home after a collision with a MiG ripped off most of its right wing.

The results of the battle over the Bekáa were electrifying—and enduring in their effect. As flown by the Syrians, Soviet aircraft and tactics had been tried and found sorely wanting. Although Soviet newspapers blamed the Syrians entirely for the calamity ("Where were the Arabs?" cried one), their sponsor was also discredited and even became the butt of jokes. Example: A Syrian general, upon

being told by his Soviet counterpart that his country had been given the Russians' best surface-to-air missiles, replied that what he really needed was some good surface-to-air missiles.

Within a week after the debacle, Colonel General Yevgeny Yurasov, first deputy commander of the Soviet Air Defense Forces, led a delegation to Damascus in quest of an explanation. Three others followed, and more than a year passed before Colonel V. Dubrov, a leading Soviet Air Force analyst, wrote a searching assessment of the Bekáa Valley fighting. He concluded that the Israeli coordination of electronic C3I accounted for the overwhelming victory of Israeli fighters and predicted that it could "be the wave of the future." Dubrov also suggested that the new, all-aspect infrared missiles capable of killing from any angle would profoundly affect the dogfight's emphasis on the tail chase. Wrote Dubrov: "Forward-hemisphere attacks, without transitioning to the maneuvering phase, were episodes heralding the future, but were not typical fighter tactics" of old. Dubrov noted, moreover, "the freedom gained from splitting the fighters away from the direct support of the larger formation of bombers. Since they are no longer subordinated to the strike group, they can perform not only defensive but also offensive combat."

Others of the world's air forces drew similar conclusions from the

A false dawn glows over West Beirut following a withering night bombardment by combined Israeli forces during the 1982 war. Earlier, the Israeli Air Force had won control of the skies over Lebanon and had also destroyed Syrian surface-to-air missiles, enabling the Israelis to strike Palestinian strongholds in the city with impunity.

Bekáa Valley experience. However, analysts pointed out that the battles there were set-piece engagements, highly localized and well rehearsed. They emphasized the dangers of equating Syrian performance with that of Soviet aviators—the 1970 shootdown of Russians over Egypt notwithstanding—or of assuming that every Soviet-trained air force would repeat the Syrian errors.

Nevertheless, Israel's air operations over Lebanon had served as the first full-scale validation of the latest-generation American technology and tactics. And in the early autumn of 1990, as American, European, and Arab forces assembled in the Saudi Arabian desert to confront Iraq, an observer wrote that in a shooting war, "The U.S. will do all it can to avoid slugging it out in prolonged ground warfare. The model for the way it hopes to fight is Israel's stunning 1982 victory over Syria's air force in Lebanon." ★

Pulse-Doppler Radar

In electronic mimicry of such skilled hunters as bats and dolphins, combat jets search out their prey by beaming energy into the ocean of air and analyzing any reflections. The probing is done with short-wavelength radio waves—hence the term *radar*, which is an acronym for "radio detection and ranging."

Since the late 1940s, jet-fighter radars have used a technique called pulse-delay ranging. This method offers an easy and precise way to determine the range of a target. But, as explained in the diagrams at right, it also has serious limitations that make it less than ideal for air-superiority fighters such as the F-15 Eagle.

From faint echoes returning at the speed of light, the Eagle's advanced radar system can spot aircraft approaching through darkness a hundred miles away, unerringly track the target during the high-G ballet of a dogfight, and perform complex geometric calculations to ensure that a burst of cannon fire crosses an enemy's course at exactly the right instant.

The radio waves that underlie all these feats are sent outward from a hydraulically steered antenna about three feet in diameter and located in the nose of the plane. Most of the energy is transmitted in a conical beam about three degrees wide (the narrowness concentrates the radar's power and provides high resolution). When searching for other aircraft, the beam scans back and forth in a pattern determined by the pilot. At the push of a button, it will fasten on a particular target to orchestrate an attack.

The beam's energy, like that of any radar, is delivered in pulses, enabling a single antenna to serve both as a transmitter and—during the intervals between pulses—as a receiver. To improve detection performance under different conditions, the radar system can shift its pulse rate, called the pulse-repetition frequency, or PRF. And instead of the low PRF used in pulse-delay sets, the F-15's radar offers the pilot a choice of two PRF categories—known simply as medium and high—that together extend from tens of thousands of pulses per second to hundreds of thousands.

PULSE-DELAY RANGING

The time a pulse takes to travel to a target and back reveals range, but only if the echo of a target at the radar's maximum range has time to return before another pulse is emitted. Such is the situation in the chart below. Blue squares trace the passage of four radar pulses out to a target at maximum range and back (time is plotted vertically and indicated by the running clock). The interval between pulses is matched to the radar's range to ensure that pulses always travel from radar to target *(red reflection)* and back *(red clock)* before another pulse is emitted. If this condition is not met, range cannot be gauged, as shown at right for a radar of longer range. Pulses repeat sooner than a maximum-range echo can return. An unresolvable ambiguity arises, as echoes of a pulse from targets close-in arrive at the same time as echoes from earlier pulses arrive from more distant targets *(faint red reflections)*—and vice versa. Lowering the PRF would solve the problem, but doing so degrades a radar's powers of discernment to an unacceptable degree.

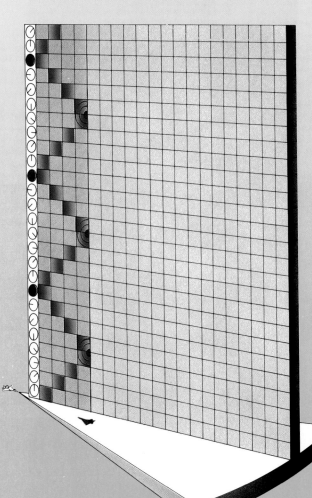

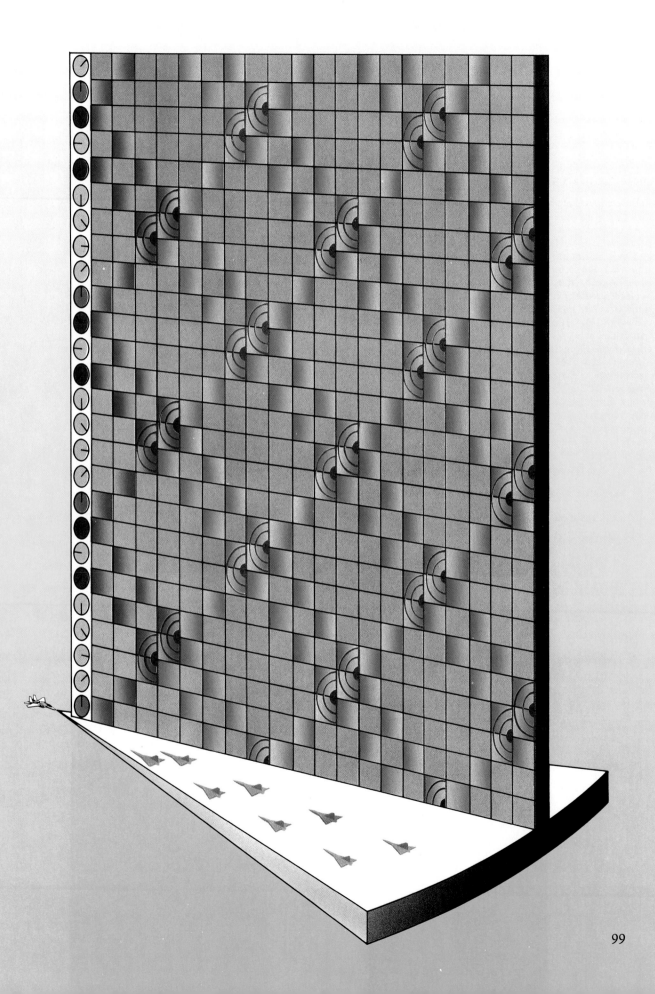

FREQUENCY MODULATION RANGING

In the chart at right, the radar operating at high PRF spends equal time transmitting and receiving. Pulses are sent out according to a repeating schedule of progressively increasing frequencies (indicated by changing colors). The time needed to complete this schedule is adjusted to the radar's maximum range so that all echoes from a pulse of any frequency will have returned before another pulse of that frequency is transmitted. With so many pulses and frequencies going out and returning, a problem arises that is most clearly illustrated with multiple targets that differ only slightly in range. As shown here, the echo from an early blue pulse reflected from the more distant aircraft arrives simultaneously with a later, yellow-pulse echo from the nearer plane. The radar averages the mixed return, obtaining a single frequency that accurately reflects the position of neither target. This frequency averaging accounts for most of the radar's range inaccuracy while operating at high PRF.

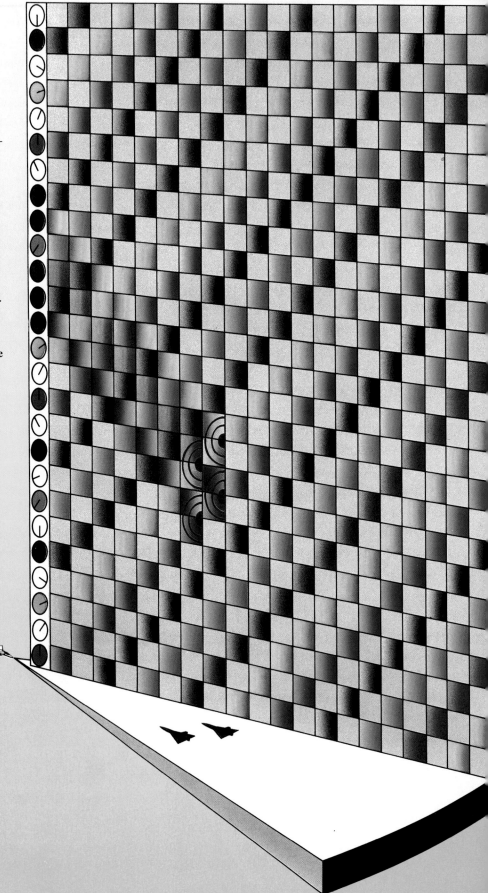

High PRF for Long-Range Detection

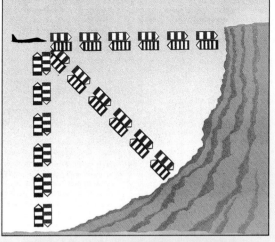

The Doppler shift of ground clutter varies between zero and an amount attributable to aircraft speed. Echoes from a point directly below the plane—a point that, for an instant, is moving neither toward or away from the jet—show no shift. Maximum shift occurs only when flying directly toward terrain.

In search mode, the F-15's radar operates at 300,000 pulses per second. Radiating more pulses raises total power, illuminating targets more brightly and strengthening echoes. Range ambiguities would be rampant, however, were it not for a companion technique called frequency-modulation (FM) ranging. As shown at left, FM ranging uses a schedule of pulses, each sent at a slightly higher frequency than the preceding one. By checking the frequency of an echo, the radar can gauge the time since sending the pulse and, from that, calculate range.

As explained on the facing page, however, FM ranging has an error of five percent or so. Accordingly, high PRF is used mainly to detect a threatening presence at great distances, where such an error is acceptable.

Putting the radar in a fast-moving aircraft complicates FM ranging because of the so-called Doppler shift, which affects radar echoes as it does a train whistle's pitch when the train approaches or recedes into the distance. To compensate, the radar considers both target speed, which it measures, and the speed of the F-15.

The Doppler effect is not all nuisance. It is vital to the radar's ability to look down and see oncoming targets that would be lost to a pulse-delay radar in bright echoes from the earth, called ground clutter.

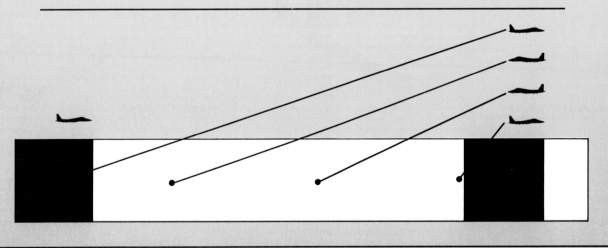

Looking down, a pulse-Doppler radar can isolate a target from ground clutter as long as the target is moving toward the radar, even if slowly. In the illustration above, ground clutter appears as tinted blocks. The topmost plane is traveling in the same direction as the radar but slower; target-echo Doppler shifts fall within the range of those for terrain echoes and can-not be separated from them. The second target from the top is heading toward the radar, as is the third. Their shifts lie outside the ground clutter region. The bottom plane is traveling away from the radar at more than twice its speed, creating a Doppler shift that also falls outside ground clutter. (As a practical matter, the F-15's radar does not display such targets; a rapidly fleeing enemy poses little threat.) A target closing at great speed would be lost in the right-hand block of ground clutter. Its position depends on radar PRF, so designers chose a PRF high enough so that this ground clutter falls where it would obscure only targets moving faster than any aircraft will fly for many years.

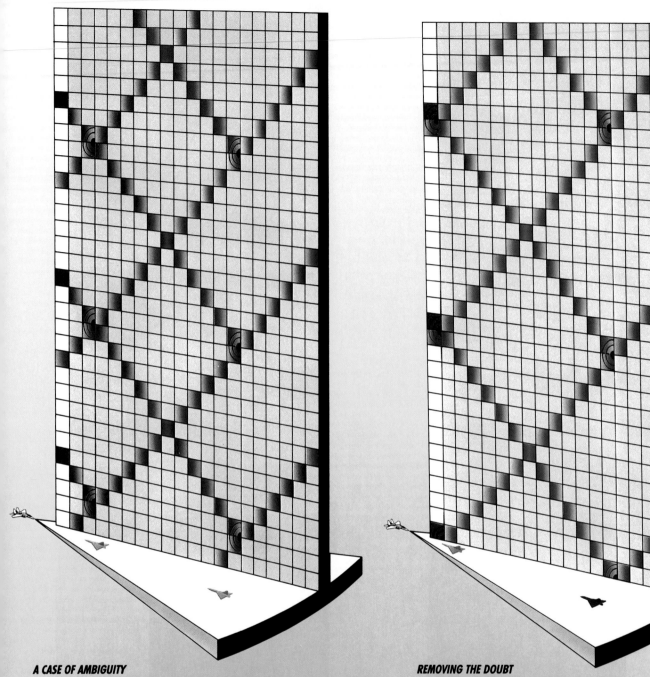

A CASE OF AMBIGUITY

In medium PRF, pulses repeat too rapidly for all echoes from any one pulse to arrive at the radar before another goes out. Each pulse *(blue)* is followed by a listening period measured by ten squares on the vertical axis. Arriving echoes *(red squares)* could be coming from two possible ranges *(red vertical lines)*, depending on which pulse produced which echo.

REMOVING THE DOUBT

To resolve the range ambiguity, the radar switches to a second, slightly lower PRF with a listening period indicated by the twelve squares between each outgoing pulse. Although an ambiguity remains, one of the possible ranges has shifted toward the radar. But the other remains unchanged, signaling that it represents the true distance to the target. When closely spaced targets are detected, other ambiguities may arise, but these can be removed by switching between three PRFs rather than two.

Medium PRF for Greater Precision

As a potentially hostile aircraft comes nearer, the range error found in FM ranging becomes unacceptable. At distances less than forty miles or so, therefore, the radar is usually operated in medium PRF, about 10,000 pulses per second.

The longer interval between pulses gives the radar not only the accuracy of a pulse-delay device, but also its undesirable range ambiguities *(pages 100-101)*. To resolve these ambiguities, the radar switches between multiple PRFs, all near each other in the medium range *(left)*.

Besides range ambiguity, medium PRF has a second unwanted side effect on ground-clutter Doppler. Medium PRF makes ground clutter repeat more often, increasing the chance that a target will be lost in these echoes. As shown below, the solution is to switch briefly between three different PRFs, all of which also fall in the medium part of the PRF spectrum.

Depending on the radar's PRF, a high-speed jet fighter could be masked by blocks of ground clutter that appear closer together as PRF is lowered. The solution is to illuminate the target with beams of different PRFs. Doing so shifts the ground clutter so that even a target with a closing speed falling in overlapping ground clutter at two PRFs will be unmasked at the third.

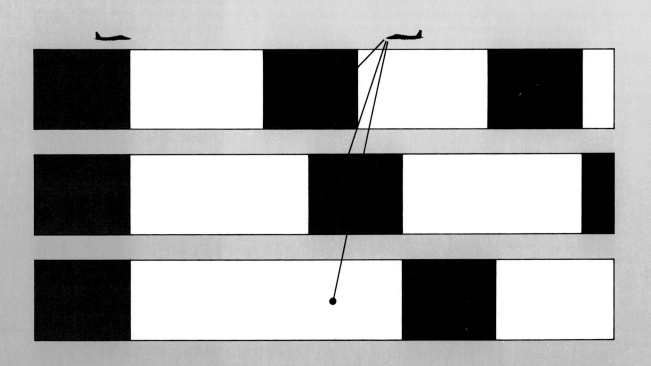

What the Pilot Sees

A pulse-Doppler radar is an electronic marvel, carrying out a prodigious number of calculations and signal manipulations at lightning speed. Not the least of its many tasks is to keep the pilot fully informed—from the moment of first radar contact through the firing of a missile or a gun—as shown by the radarscope illustrations at right.

Horizontal range lines on the screen fall at five-, ten-, or twenty-mile intervals depending on the mode in which the radar is operating. Vertical lines spaced ten degrees apart represent angles left and right of the antenna's centerline. As shown on a scale along the bottom of the scope, the antenna can be pointed to look left or right of the aircraft. A scale on the left of the screen reports how many degrees up or down the antenna is pointing.

At the top left corner in most modes of operation is the range of altitudes, in thousands of feet, covered by the antenna. The number above the upper right corner is the value of the top range line. At the lower corners appear the F-15's position in latitude and longitude; between these coordinates, the radar displays the plane's groundspeed and true airspeed. Directly above the latitude, the scope informs the pilot of the radar beam's progress through its scan pattern and whether the device is operating in high or medium PRF.

When tracking a single target to shoot at it *(bottom screen, far right)*, the radar begins to display other target data and to supply steering cues that will maximize the chances of a kill.

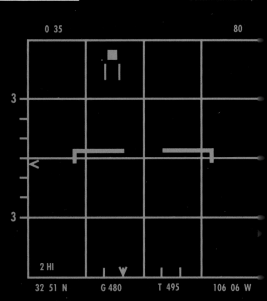

A first look. Operating in the high PRF search mode, an F-15's radar detects a target at a distance of about seventy-five miles—a quarter of the distance between the eighty-mile, maximum range line at the top of the scope and the sixty-mile line below it. The bogey appears as a square; two vertical lines form a cursor called the target acquisition symbol that the pilot uses later to tell the radar which target to lock onto.

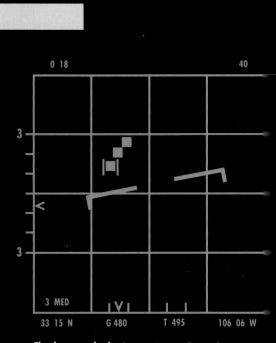

The threat resolved. Three minutes later the target is within thirty miles, and the pilot switches to medium PRF for a better look. Superior range resolution in medium PRF reveals the presence of three bogeys.

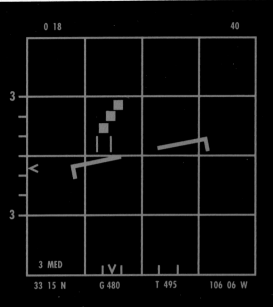

Setting up for an attack. The pilot tells the radar that the nearest bogey will be the target. He does so by pushing a button on the throttle left, right, up, or down to move the cursor to the target. Pressing, then releasing, the button establishes radar lock.

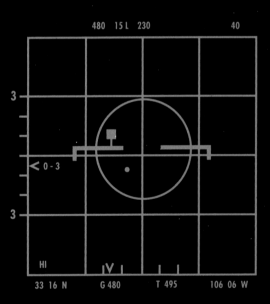

Angling for a shot. The target's airspeed (480) and compass heading (230) appear at the top of the screen. Between them is the aspect angle, the pilot's position relative to the target. Here the angle is 150 degrees left as measured clockwise from the foe's tail: The F-15 is at the enemy's eleven o'clock position. A line added to the target symbol shows that the enemy and the F-15 are flying in opposite directions. Target altitude—300 feet here—appears next to the pointer on the left of the screen.

A circle appears on both the radarscope and on the aircraft's head-up display. The pilot can launch a missile as long as he keeps a spot called a steering dot *(lower left quadrant)* inside the ring by steering toward it. Dot position and circle size vary according to the radar's analysis of the missile's ability to track the target.

Graduate Degrees in Fighter Tactics

From behind an oxygen mask and a visor to cut the glare of the sun, a radar intercept officer (RIO) scans the sky for "bandits" from the backseat of an F-14. In an emergency, pulling the striped handles behind his head jettisons the Tomcat's canopy and fires the RIO's ejection seat, which automatically opens his parachute. The small devices alongside his shoulder-harness buckles release the chute in seawater, preventing him from being dragged under.

An old military adage states: "You fight like you train." It is universally applicable—in everything, always. And in the late 1960s and early 1970s, the United States Air Force and Navy set out to make certain that never again would they perform as poorly as they had in Southeast Asia. "The results we got against a rinky-dink power like North Vietnam," recalls a veteran of the air-to-air combat in that war, "were not pleasing." The next fight for air superiority—whether it unfolds in the skies above Europe, Korea, Iraq, or in some other, as yet unanticipated, venue—will find American aviators far better prepared for their adversary.

Air Force combat training reaches its epitome in the Red Flag exercises held five times a year at Nellis Air Force Base in the Nevada desert, ten miles north of Las Vegas. Sooner or later, virtually every Air Force fighter crewman becomes a player in the games called World War. For it is as close to war fighting as the Air Force can make it; everything on both sides comes into action, the entire roster of U.S. tactical aircraft and techniques against a mock enemy, trained to mimic potential foes in every detail—from the capabilities of their aircraft to tactics and temperament, including the dirty tricks the enemy can be expected to play. The model has always been the Soviet Air Force, and for good reason. Until the late 1980s, it not only seemed to pose a significant threat in its own right, but it had also trained client air forces around the world.

Red Flag's objective revolves around a second axiom of combat that commanders there are fond of quoting: Inexperience kills. Statistics show that a pilot who lives through his first ten missions has learned enough to stand a good chance of surviving the war. Red Flag gives aviators an opportunity to fly those ten missions before being challenged by a real enemy firing real bullets and missiles.

In addition to Red Flag and a variety of other "flag" exercises that train pilots in every kind of aerial operation, the U.S. Air Force conducts a number of fighter weapons schools that concentrate on air-to-air combat. Perhaps the best known fighter weapons school, however, belongs to the Navy. It is called Top Gun.

Only the fleet's most promising pilots are invited to participate. Based at Miramar Naval Air Station, near San Diego, California, Top Gun isolates the fighter duel from other aspects of aerial warfare. Pilots fight to the absolute limits of their abilities against expert instructors in aircraft that closely match the characteristics of MiGs and Sukhois. Success at Top Gun convinces a pilot that he can beat the best Soviet flier who ever lived, and when he returns to the fleet, he teaches his squadronmates how to do the same. "We like to think we're better pilots than anyone else in the world," but not, says a graduate, "because we're supermen. We have the same reaction times and motor skills as anyone else—but because we train harder and longer. The more air combat you're involved in, the better you get. After a while, you don't waste time thinking about what you have to do. You just do it."

Games at the Playground

In unison with his flight leader, the F-15 pilot advances his throttle into the afterburner position, unleashing from the Eagle's twin engines nearly 48,000 pounds of thrust that press him into the seat. The aircraft surges forward, accelerating within seconds to 170 knots, flying speed. At the same instant, both of the fliers ease back on the stick, and the Eagles become airborne. Gear up. Flaps up. By the time the planes clear the

Engines running, F-16s of the 169th Tactical Fighter Squadron, South Carolina Air National Guard, undergo a final check before taking off on a Red Flag training mission. Each plane's crew chief, standing in view of his pilot, signals when all is in order for the jet to taxi to the runway.

overrun at the end of the runway, they are at 500 feet, banking hard north toward Fossil Ridge, thence out Sally Corridor to join up with other elements over the dry bed of Texas Lake. The day's assignment is to fly CAP for a fleet of strike aircraft. Another Red Flag exercise is under way.

In the years just after Vietnam, a U.S. Air Force colonel named Richard M. Suter visited U.S. fighter bases around the world, asking aircrews how their training might be improved. In long bull sessions often lasting far into the night, with notes sometimes scribbled on bar napkins, Suter found a common theme: U.S. training, excellent as far as it went, stopped short of preparing pilots for war; it taught pilots to be masters of technique but not how to prevail against a skilled and determined adversary. Incredibly, Suter at one point found a squadron in England that had not flown a single air-to-air training mission in three years; the crews were simply "flying around the flagpole," logging hours but making little progress as warriors.

Suter's answer—and that of many other

thoughtful officers—was to extend the Air Force's training program so that it would give young pilots realistic combat experience without a shooting war. In 1975, Suter got the ear of General Robert J. Dixon, boss of the Tactical Air Command, and within a few months Red Flag was born.

American fliers would be exposed to the ways of whatever air force they might be expected to fight. They would become familiar with the characteristics of every Soviet fighter aircraft, beginning with the 5,000 MiG-21 Fishbeds and 3,000 MiG-23 Floggers that were in service with dozens of nations. In time, their studies would extend to the new and dangerous Su-27 Flanker and the equally lethal MiG-29 Fulcrum already exported by the hundreds to a dozen countries, including Iraq, Syria, North Korea, and Cuba. The pilots would learn the capabilities of enemy radars and weapons. By flying against western aircraft similar in perfor-

Pertinent Advice from an Ace of the Past

The most renowned name in all of air combat is that of Manfred von Richthofen, Germany's legendary Red Baron who in World War I shot down eighty enemy planes before himself perishing in battle. Yet Richthofen's acknowledged superior was his friend and mentor, Oswald Boelcke. Until his death in 1916, Boelcke, with forty victories, reigned supreme as the German Air Service's foremost ace, its premier aerial strategist, teacher, and combat leader. And it was the great Boelcke who handed down eight commandments of air-combat tactics—maxims that remain pertinent even in the supersonic, radar-and-missile environment of aerial warfare in the 1990s.

The Boelcke Dicta:
Try to secure advantages before attacking. If possible keep the sun behind you. The upper hand lies with the pilot who engages from a position of strength deriving from greater numbers, higher speed, and the element of surprise.

Always carry through an attack when you have started it. A flier who loses his nerve and breaks off before the battle is won provides his enemy with an opportunity to turn the tables.

Fire only at close range and only when your opponent is properly in your sights. For Boelcke, the ideal machine-gun range was twenty yards, where it was hard to miss. Even with today's radar gunsights

mance to Soviet models, American pilots would learn how fast and how maneuverable their potential foes might be, how to exploit weaknesses, and how to counter strengths. Above all, they would come to understand the opposing pilots in their level of training and in their tactics.

For aviators who may be called upon to hazard their lives in the air space over the Saudi Arabian desert or the mountains of Iraq's Jebel Sinjar, Nellis offers an ideal training ground. The huge reservation sprawls over an area only slightly smaller than Switzerland—10 million acres of mesquite and sagebrush populated by rattlesnakes, tarantulas, and thousands of mustangs that live off the sparse vegetation.

Exercises are restricted to about three million acres on three ranges that together constitute Redland. This make-believe country is forever at war with the United States, its grim terrain freckled with thousands of targets in about fifty types, including some 200 ply-

and powerful cannon that can reach more than a mile, it remains true that the shorter the range the better.

*Always keep your eye on your opponent. Modern radar can detect an adversary long before he can be seen, but once a pilot sights the target, he must keep it in view at all times. As they say at Red Flag and Top Gun: Lose sight, lose the fight.

*In any form of attack, it is important to assail your opponent from behind. The long-range, radar-orchestrated, head-to-head joust with all-aspect missiles may be the preferred opening gambit for U.S. pilots in the 1990s. But after the first pass, there is nothing like being firmly on an enemy's tail. An attacker has time to make

sure of the next missile attack and to go with guns if the missile fails. Something else: The enemy cannot fire back.

*If your opponent dives on you, do not try to evade his onslaught but fly to meet it. Again the best policy, even against an opponent armed with all-aspect missiles. It is easier to defeat a missile that is coming head-on than to dodge one racing for your tailpipe. It also is easier to take the offensive.

*When over the enemy's lines, never forget your own line of retreat. Aside from keeping constant track of his position, a pilot should think ahead about fuel supply and enemy ground-to-air missiles and aircraft formations that might block escape

routes. In a narrow, north-south arena such as Vietnam, for example, U.S. pilots would run in from west to east—thereby making it easier to reach the sea if they got in trouble.

*Attack on principle in groups of four or six. When the fight breaks up into a series of single combats, take care that several do not go for one opponent. Boelcke originated the idea of section tactics, two planes acting in concert against an adversary and guarding each other against surprise attack. And if two was good, four or six offered still greater firepower and an increased defensive outlook. If the fight becomes a series of individual actions, pilots should be careful not to get in one another's way.

wood or polystyrene tanks and other armored vehicles belonging to the fictional 108th Guards Tank Army. Junked aircraft, many of Korean War vintage, are parked on mock airstrips that have been scratched in the sand. An industrial complex consists of a collection of ramshackle wooden buildings held together by baling wire. A scrap-metal train sits motionless on a sham railroad track leading into a tunnel that is in reality a shallow hole gouged into the side of a mountain. Telephone poles painted white and laid end to end resemble an oil pipeline. Protecting these installations is an awesome array of dummy AAA and SAM batteries that would, if they were genuine, make flying over this battlefield a hazardous enterprise.

Participants commonly call this assemblage of fakery the Playground, but it all looks real enough to the pilot of a Blue Force F-111F fighter-bomber jinking toward his target at 500 knots. The goal of the visiting aviators of Blue Force is to obliterate the targets on the ground, first with bombs and rockets simulated by radio signals and later with searing metal and high explosives.

And so, every ten weeks or so, players from all points of the compass gather at Nellis, arriving in their own aircraft. The tarmac becomes jammed with C-130 transports and tiny OH-58 Kiowa scout helicopters, eye-in-the-sky E-3 Sentry AWACS aircraft to direct the air battle and swing-wing EF-111 Ravens packed with electronic jamming gear, A-10 Thunderbolt II antitank planes, F-111F fighter-bombers ready to streak across the desert a hundred feet above the ground, F-4G Phantom Wild Weasels for knocking out antiaircraft radars, even some of Strategic Air Command's B-52s capable of carrying not only nuclear weapons but scores of conventional bombs or air-launched cruise missiles of unprecedented range and accuracy.

Besides Americans, British pilots may show up flying Jaguars and Tornadoes, and French airmen come in Mirage 2000s. Israeli fliers bring their Kfirs, and Canadian aviators arrive in U.S.-built F/A-18 Hornets. Even the U.S. Navy participates in the exercises at Redland from time to time.

For the attack aircraft to do their job, however, air-superiority fighters must somehow wrest control of the skies from Red Force aggressors. Some of the Blue Force pilots are experienced aviators, returning to Nellis to sharpen their skills for perhaps the dozenth time. But others are brash young men who wear their shapeless gray-green flight suits as if they were shining armor. These sometimes cocky neophytes can be in for a surprise. In the words of one Red Flag officer, early encounters with the aggressors will make most of these young fliers return from Redland "with eyes as big as saucers."

Red Flag scenarios differ from exercise to exercise, but the core unit—the one around which each script revolves—is always a fighter wing of the Tactical Air Command. And, since fighter wings ordinarily consist of three squadrons, the six weeks the airmen spend at Red Flag are broken into three segments, giving each squadron a two-week turn at center stage, planning missions involving the other two. Because Red Flag stands down on weekends, each aircrew has ten days in which they push themselves and their aircraft to their limits.

For Blue Force, the day begins with a 7:30 briefing called the AM Go. In a building at Nellis, an ample auditorium fills with pilots and crews. The excitement, punctuated by lively chatter, is almost palpable. Hands arc through the air in the language by which pilots habitually describe aerial maneuvers. It is all symptomatic of an underlying tension. According to a first-timer, "You sense it when you walk in the door. Everybody's under the gun."

The men take seats for a full report on the ground situation in the mock war being fought, a review of the rules of engagement, and a detailed explanation of the day's strikes. Afterward, the aircrews sort out into groups. Consulting with the leaders of various flight elements is the day's designated "Warlord," a player assigned to coordinate commanders in the group's execution of operations orders issued by Red Flag planners.

The Warlord may, for example, be a highflying F-15 pilot who is confronted for the first time with the problems of putting together a mission involving F-4 Wild Weasel SAM suppressors, EF-111 Raven jammers, and A-10 Thunderbolt tank busters, all coordinated by AWACS. The Warlord—and every other player, for that matter—can consult thirty thick books that cover every nuance of aircraft performance, with graphs showing fuel consumption for various bombloads, the number of bombs needed to ensure destruction of a target, and a wealth of other data.

Of particular value are face-to-face planning discussions between

Monitoring the simulated combat that unfolds at Nellis Air Force Base in Nevada—and at more than a dozen similar aerial-warfare arenas in North America, Europe, and Asia—is a system known as ACMI—Air Combat Maneuvering Instrumentation system. (The Navy calls it TACTS—Tactical Aircrew Combat Training System.) Designed and built by the Cubic Corporation of San Diego, California, ACMI enables moderators on the ground to follow the actions of as many as thirty-six aircraft as they tangle in mock aerial combat above the training range.

Fitted to each plane taking part in an exercise is an instrument pod roughly the dimensions of a Sidewinder air-to-air missile.

Linked electronically to the plane's weapons systems, the pod keeps track of flight data such as altitude, speed, heading, and other factors that define the motion of the aircraft. The instrument pod also senses when a pilot squeezes the trigger that in an actual fight would fire his cannon or launch a missile. From such information, high-speed computers on the ground can judge at any instant during an encounter where real cannon shells would strike or whether a missile would be likely to home on its intended target.

The computers receive aircraft data by way of a network of radio relay stations, as illustrated on these pages. The process begins at the control center *(bottom right)*,

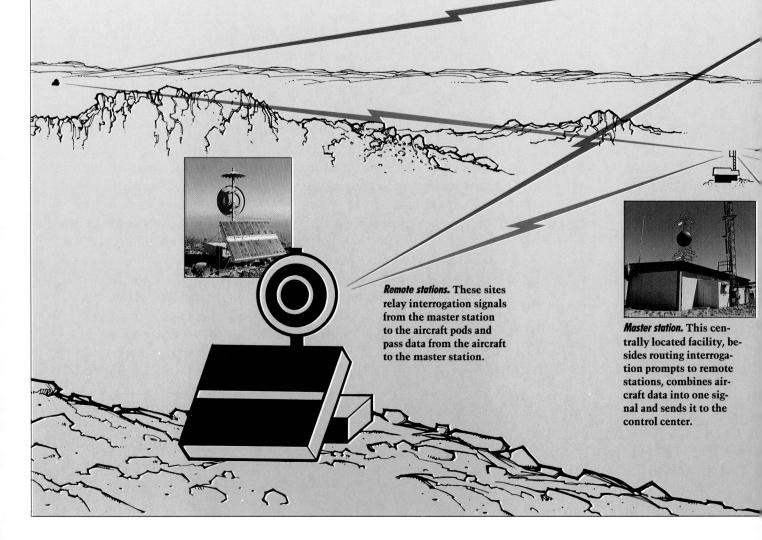

Remote stations. These sites relay interrogation signals from the master station to the aircraft pods and pass data from the aircraft to the master station.

Master station. This centrally located facility, besides routing interrogation prompts to remote stations, combines aircraft data into one signal and sends it to the control center.

Instrument pod. Mounted on a Sidewinder launch rail, the nine-foot-long cylinder receives interrogation signals from the remote stations and responds with flight and weapons data.

which initiates an interrogation signal for the instrument pod on each aircraft. The signals *(green)*, each coded with a number that addresses it to a particular pod, go first to a centrally located relay station called the master station, which retransmits the messages *(blue)* to remote stations spotted around the perimeter of the exercise area. These in turn broadcast the signals *(red)* to the aircraft.

When a pod receives an interrogation signal with the appropriate code number, it replies with a burst of data that all the remote stations relay to the master station. From there, the information passes to the computers at the control center. This cycle is repeated as often as ten times a second. The computers save the data and, working at 18 million operations per second or more, convert it into images that show action developing virtually as it is happening.

An observer called the range training officer (RTO) monitors the twisting, turning aircraft. Among other duties, he has the responsibility for telling a pilot when he has been shot down so that he and his adversary can break off their engagement and perhaps begin another.

In debriefing sessions after the day's flying, a pilot can see his performance replayed from every conceivable angle and perspective—from his own seat, or from that of the pilot who shot him down *(pages 134-139)*.

Control center. Banks of computers in these buildings originate interrogation signals for aircraft. The computers also process data as it arrives from the master station and display the action on monitors used to follow exercises in progress and for debriefing the pilots.

pilots of different aircraft with diverse experience. "If you've never had to talk to those guys about how they go about their business," a Red Flag officer has explained, "you don't have a good understanding of what they do. And that lack of understanding is going to be a severe detriment if you go to war."

As planning proceeds, flight leaders and wingmen, pilots and weapons systems operators—wizzos—make "contracts" among themselves. These oral agreements settle the formations and tactics they will use in battle. Pilots in a flight of four Eagles slated for combat air patrol, for instance, may decide that the flight leader and his wingman will go high while the other two fighters will deploy low, so that only one pair of aircraft at a time will be visible to enemy radar. Such coordination is necessary. In the event that enemy jammers disrupt communications between planes, pilots flying together will know in advance what to expect from the others in their flight.

The details of what happens at Redland during any specific exercise are classified, but there is nothing secret about the general course of events. Depending on the mission, the Blue Force will launch eighteen strike aircraft plus a dozen support sorties—Wild Weasels, Raven electronic warfare aircraft, an AWACS, and tankers. Another twenty or so fighters will fill an air-to-air role, either escorting the strike aircraft or crisscrossing the skies above them as CAP, whose job is to shoot down enemy fighters before they can threaten the fighter-bombers. To oppose the Blue Force, Redland will send up a dozen or two defending fighters, often supported by electronic warfare planes to jam Blue's radio transmissions. Overall, somewhere between seventy and one hundred planes may be roaring around Redland at the same time—an awesome amount of fast-flying metal in an air space only forty miles wide by ninety miles long. In the confusion lies much of the realism. Air-to-air encounters can be expected to take place not in isolation but as part of a campaign with wider objectives than shooting the enemy out of the sky.

Keeping track of all this activity is a computerized scorekeeper on the ground called ACMI *(pages 114-115)*. From the aircraft participating in the exercise, it gathers or calculates such critical data as altitude, airspeed, range between aircraft, angle of attack, G-load, closing velocity, and the results of simulated cannon firings and missile launches in air-to-air engagements.

ACMI is not an air-traffic control system that keeps planes out of each other's way, so exercise or not, the flying is dangerous; during Red Flag's early years there were thirty-three fatal accidents, twenty-three of them caused by collisions with the ground. So pilots need to recognize, a Red Flag commander once explained, "that the biggest threat in this Redland territory out here is the ground or hitting another airplane. It is still simulated war, and there is nothing at Nellis worth dying for."

For that reason, certain rules of engagement are imposed. For example, players are forbidden to fight below 300 feet during their first week in Redland; after that, they are allowed to venture as low as 100 feet—but only if their commander certifies in writing that they are competent at that height.

Inevitably, the rules cause some gripes, especially from aggressors, who argue that the prohibitions hinder them from realistically simulating tactics of potential adversaries. Soviet fighter pilots in a dogfight, for example, are partial to head-on attacks to take advantage of the superior range of their 30-mm cannon compared to the 20-mm guns in most U.S. fighter planes. Because of the obvious danger of collisions, however, front-quarter gun assaults are banned at Red Flag.

In addition to standing rules, restrictions may be imposed according to different scenarios. Weapons for one day's air-to-air dueling may be guns only. Another day, an 8,000-foot combat ceiling may be imposed, with transgressors being declared dead. Some other morning, the AWACS radar planes that give Blue Force a significant advantage may be arbitrarily ordered to shut down. "There's only one trouble with AWACS," says a Red Flag officer. "It's so good the guys rapidly stop looking around." But with the plane out of the picture, Blue Force pilots, to avoid disaster, must revert quickly to reliance on their wits and their own eyes.

From the time that a referee radios "Fight's on!" until the participating aircraft return to base, a mission over Redland may last no more than an hour, yet it can seem an eternity. And when the exhausted players, their flight suits soaked with the sweat of anxiety, return to the base at Nellis, they go through the most sobering part of their day: the debriefing. During these sessions, which may last as long as three hours, aircrews can watch ACMI replay the events of the morning's exercise in exhaustive detail—every turn, every dive, every roll—on a large monitor. A pilot who shot down

117

his target can see what he almost did wrong that might have reversed the results. A victim can appreciate his errors and try not to repeat them next time out.

And therein lies the value of mock combat over Redland: There a man can live to fight another day; in a real war he might not have lived to celebrate that watershed tenth mission.

Soviet Tactics in the Skies over Nevada

Over the portal of a low, beige structure that seemed eager to blend into the vast expanse of surrounding desert blazed an emblem: a huge red star centered in the reticle of a fighter-aircraft gunsight. Inside, the walls were alight with red flags. Banners and posters carried Cyrillic letters proclaiming "Death to the Enemy."

Throughout the 1980s, this building was headquarters to a fighter squadron. From the colonel down, the pilots all wore red star patches on their right shoulders. Their aircraft were garbed in the camouflage schemes favored by the USSR, its Warsaw Pact allies, and various Third World client states: dark gray on gray for fighters operating over the Soviet motherland, brown on green for Central Europe, light brown on dark brown for desert climes such as Libya and Syria. On the planes' noses were painted foot-high, double-digit numbers that identify Soviet military aircraft.

All these details, however authentic, were nonetheless far from genuine. The headquarters building was one of many that sprawl across the vastness of Nellis Air Force Base in Nevada. The aircraft, paint jobs notwithstanding, were in fact front-line American F-16 Falcons. The pilots were members not of a Soviet fighter squadron but of the 64th Aggressor Squadron, arguably the finest collection of pilots in the U.S. Air Force.

For eighteen years, the 64th was the heart of the opposition force in the Red Flag exercises. They were the instructors whose mission was to emulate a potential adversary in every way possible. "The idea," said an aggressor colonel, is to "do the best we can to learn all the plays that we think are going to be run against us by the next team we face, and we run plays against our 'varsity,' our front-line fighters, trying to expose the weaknesses in the adversary's plan and

An F-16 from Nellis's 64th Aggressor Squadron sports the olive-and-tan camouflage favored by one-time Warsaw Pact air forces. During the 64th's heyday, small detachments of these aircraft, which mimicked the tactics of Soviet-trained forces, visited F-15 wings at their home bases to sharpen the Eagle pilots' air-combat skills.

118

also our own, thereby removing as many surprises as possible."

Budget restraints and changes in the fighter tactics of potential foes have caused the Air Force to disband the 64th. But dissolving the unit cannot subtract from its value in teaching novice fighter pilots the finer points of air-to-air combat. Even in demise, its spirit and at least some of its practices will endure. For whatever the future course of U.S. Air Force air-combat training, some pilot or another will have to play the aggressor if the United States is to retain its edge in the air.

For thirty weeks a year, the 64th's aggressors played their role to the hilt. To the best of their abilities, which were considerable, and their training, which was very special, these pilots thought like Soviet airmen, flew planes that simulated Soviet fighters, and applied Soviet tactics. To join the 64th, a pilot had to have flown at least 500 hours —equivalent to three years' experience—in fighter aircraft. But the norm was closer to 1,000 hours, and one commander had racked up 4,000. During a stringent selection process, applicants were judged not only by their superlative skills and extensive experience but also on their mental maturity and teaching ability. The screening, said a Red Force officer, "weeds out the King Kongs who are just looking to notch kills."

Pilots who made the cut spent the first two weeks of a ten-week training period at the Soviet Awareness School in Washington, D.C., soaking up information about the historical, political, and cultural factors that influence Soviet fighter pilots. Next came a forty-seven-day Aggressor Tactics Instructor Course at Nellis. The flying curriculum consisted of forty-one sorties, enough to train these pilots to mimic their top-rated Soviet counterparts in every way save language. Fighting by the Soviet book often went against the grain. One pilot said, "We fly no-fooling Soviet tactics and we don't cheat on it. So we'll go out there and fly these Soviet tactics and some of them get us 'killed.' You say, 'Boy, I wouldn't do that if I was smart.' But we're not allowed to be smart."

One Soviet custom proved particularly uncomfortable for the

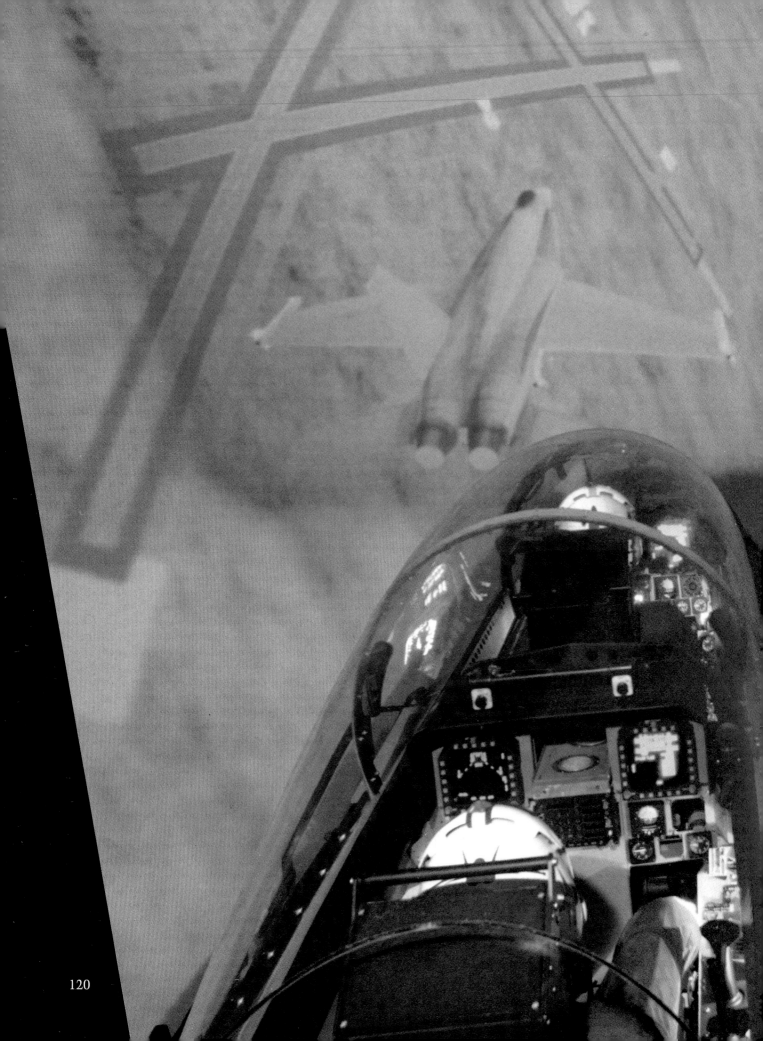

Creating a Realistic Illusion

Simulators have long been used in pilot training to reduce the costs and the dangers to men and machines. And in an era of high expenses and decreasing defense budgets, when the average American fighter pilot flies less than an hour a day in a real airplane, simulators have become all the more appealing. Moreover, these machines can offer experiences—flying a battle-damaged aircraft, for example—that would be impractical without them.

Among the most advanced simulators is the Weapons Tactics Trainer (WTT) built to train U.S. Navy and Marine fighter pilots. The WTT allows two pilots to pit themselves against each other, against adversaries generated by powerful computers that lie at the heart of the system, or against a pilot seated behind controls at the instructor's terminal.

The WTT offers an imperfect illusion of flight. But to a pilot sitting in a replica of a fighter cockpit, the fabrication is convincing enough during the stress of simulated combat to pass as genuine. To create such realism, the computers project images of aircraft and terrain, mimic the sounds of cannons and missiles firing, and even imi-

Two airmen in a replica of an F/A-18 cockpit *(left)* return to base behind the image of their flight leader after a mission flown inside a WTT flight simulator like the one diagramed below. Two hollow spheres, forty feet across, fill one end of the WTT building. Each contains a cockpit and several projectors for visual effects. Behind the domes are terminals where instructors monitor or participate in the exercise, a debrief station where past missions can be replayed, and banks of computers that generate images and correlate all visual, tactile, and aural components of the simulation in the two domes.

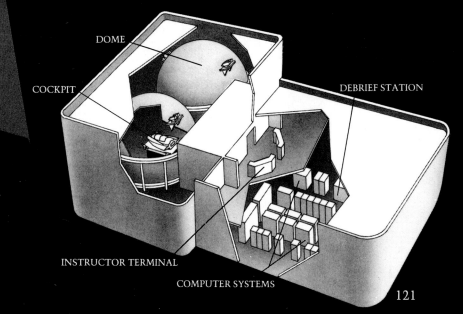

DOME

COCKPIT

DEBRIEF STATION

INSTRUCTOR TERMINAL

COMPUTER SYSTEMS

tate the turbulence of a thunderstorm—produced by a machine called a shaker, on which the cockpit is mounted.

During such maneuvers as turning, climbing, or diving, the simulator adjusts air pressure inside bladders in the back and sides of the seat and alters the tension of the shoulder harness to simulate G forces. The computer also authentically inflates the crew's G-suits as if to keep the blood from draining into their legs when the pilot banks the "aircraft" into a turn. For all its realism, however, a shaker cannot replicate the heaviness of head and limb felt in a sustained high-G maneuver. Nor can it provide the sensation of blacking out.

A WTT costs some $40 million to build, not much more than the price of a single jet fighter. And operating it is a bargain. Each hour of flight in an F/A-18, for example, costs about $2,000; in the WTT, the bill is an economical $150.

Inside each simulator dome is a replica of an F/A-18 cockpit. It is mounted on a shaker machine set into a stationary platform. The corners are fitted with computer-operated projectors that can produce an image of the aircraft being flown from the adjacent dome, as well as pictures of targets on the ground or in the air. A projector mounted outside the dome in front of the pilot shines through a hole, illuminating the back of the dome with an image of what lies behind the pilot. This view is purposely fuzzy to ease the work load on simulator computers as they adjust the images to keep up with a fighter flying hundreds of miles per hour. Two projectors cover the front half of the dome. One produces a picture similar in quality to the one thrown onto the rear of the dome. The other casts a much sharper image on a part of the dome directly in front of the pilot called the area of interest.

Russian-designed plane, had an equally short range, and was handicapped by limited radar. Both could turn—"swap ends," in fighterpilot lingo—with admirable agility. With a top speed of mach 1.6, the F-5 was as fast as the MiG-21 and, all in all, could be served up as a pretty good imitation of a Fishbed. Said one Redland pilot: "If a guy could beat an F-5, he could beat a MiG-21."

In a fight against burly F-4 Phantoms and F-15 Eagles (the Eagle's tail span exceeds the Tiger's wingspan), the small, maneuverable F-5s could put the larger planes at a disadvantage. An Eagle pilot might not see a Redland F-5 until it approached within three miles, while his opponent could pick out the F-15 as a dot in the sky from ten miles away. Being the first to sight the foe in a dogfight is often decisive, but if the F-15 pilot could spoil or evade the F-5's first pass, the Eagle's superior power would usually win out.

The game changed when the F-5s were sent out to simulate MiG-23 Floggers. A 1970s aircraft, the Flogger is known to have great speed. Yet it is short on maneuverability, unable to sustain more than five Gs in a turn. To compensate, the 64th's pilots disciplined themselves to take less than full advantage of the maneuvering ability of their F-5s, artificially limiting themselves to five-G turns.

By the late 1980s, the F-5 Tiger was no longer representative of Soviet fighters. The latest of these aircraft are single-seat, high-G planes capable of speeds greater than mach 2 and equipped with modern radar that can detect targets at great distances and pick up low-flying aircraft that ground controllers had always tracked for them. Possibly because of this improved performance, Soviet tactics seem to have become less dependent on the ground controller.

In response to these changes, the aggressors began flying the F-16 Falcon. Widely regarded as the world's best day fighter, it can pull nine Gs in a turn and has enough thrust to accelerate vertically. The Falcon can not only simulate a MiG-21 and MiG-23, it can mimic the impressive new MiG-29 Fulcrum—and perhaps the even newer Su-27 Flanker, although the capabilities of that fighter are not yet thoroughly documented. A further consequence of improved Soviet aircraft and tactics is that many more U.S. aircraft types can serve as surrogate adversaries in Red Flag and other exercises.

Perhaps the most important skill developed in aviators flying against Nellis's resident aggressors is the one that fighter pilots call situational awareness, or SA. Acquiring it demands that a pilot detect and keep track of all the aircraft that pose a threat, and he must do so in fluid circumstances where survival depends on not being surprised by the unexpected. One pilot recalled the day he saw a fighter in the distance, and before he knew it, the plane had swept around onto his tail and shot him down. It was a Navy F-14 playing aggressor, and the pilot had failed to suspect it. "I thought he was one of our F-15s. During regular training missions we don't check six much because we know that there's no one back there." Looking to the rear is a prime component of SA; failing to do so is no way to survive in combat. Said one pilot: "If your SA is stuffed away in your lunchbox, you'll get blown out of the sky every time."

Pilots learn quickly. "We'll go out there the first couple of days," an aggressor explained, "and we'll taxi on into people's six o'clock, and they won't see us." But after someone gets shot down a few times, he "starts looking over his shoulder, paying more attention to the overall threat. Ta-da! He sees us. And defeats our attack, and then all of a sudden we end up on the defensive."

It is not that this pilot had become a more skillful stick-and-rudder man. Instead, his tactics had improved and his situational awareness had soared to a point where he had become a greater threat to his adversary than his adversary was to him. By the end of two weeks at Nellis, visiting fliers generally win the mock war with Redland. "We always fight to win," explained one of the 64th Aggressor Squadron, "but our ultimate goal is to teach pilots how to beat us." Another of the squadron put it this way: "You must understand that in our business second best is dead last."

The Best versus the Best at Top Gun

Some years ago, before the thaw in United States-Soviet relations, the faculty at the Navy's Fighter Weapons School sent Christmas greetings to Russia. Directed to "Headquarters, Soviet Air Force, Attention: MiG-21 Tactics Section, Moscow, USSR," the card included a photograph of the instructors along with the following inscription: "Thinking of you and yours at this joyful Yuletide Season. Trust all is well and cozy at your fireside. If our nations ever pair off in war, check your six o'clock. We'll be there, hosing you—Top Gun."

That card, which was returned opened but unacknowledged, cap-

The A-4's gunsight, shown here centered by a Top Gun aggressor on the A-4 of his flight leader, places the pilot at a disadvantage in a gun attack. Only one generation removed from World War II gunsights, it has no radar to calculate lead—how far ahead of a turning adversary to aim. As a poor substitute, it displays a set of aiming circles that offer the pilot minimal assistance in judging lead, which he must then dial manually into the gunsight.

tures the character of fighter pilots. As a group, they tend to be combative overachievers—intelligent, brash to the point of being juvenile at times, and supremely confident. "If you know the best fighter pilot in the world, and he ain't you," said one of the breed, "then you shouldn't be a fighter pilot."

Of the U.S. Navy's aviators who fit this description, Top Gun takes the best and turns them into world beaters. To be sure, the Navy has various fleet defense programs—one of them is called Strike—that more or less parallel the Air Force's Red Flag exercises and involve war fighting in a maritime environment. Top Gun, however, is pure aerial combat. Until the very last mission, when everyone celebrates graduation with a simulated Alpha Strike—a raid involving thirty to forty aircraft of various types—there are few Redland scenarios, and there are no Soviet-style ground controllers or tactics. Flying aircraft that replicate Soviet-built equipment—at first F-5E Tigers and nimble A-4 Skyhawks, now slightly modified F-16 Fighting Falcons—Top

Gun instructors spend almost all their time aloft hassling with their students in the skies over the air-combat maneuvering (ACM) ranges at Miramar Naval Air Station a few miles to the north of San Diego, California.

Top Gun originated in 1968 in response to the report by Captain Frank W. Ault that documented appalling deficiencies in air-to-air weapons and the training of aviators to use them. The school succeeded so brilliantly that it became a separate command in 1972. For five weeks five times a year, a dozen of the Navy's thirty F-14 Tomcat and F/A-18 Hornet squadrons are each invited to select an aircrew for Top Gun. The pilot—and his backseater if he flies the F-14—can be designated unilaterally by the squadron skipper or as the result of a squadron flyoff with Top Gun as the prize. However the choice is made, it is a signal honor, a reward for excellence.

Most of the students are approaching their thirties. Each pilot and radar intercept officer (RIO) has no fewer than 500 hours in Tomcats or Hornets, and at least one six-month cruise aboard an aircraft carrier. They are experts, and they are at Top Gun to learn the innermost secrets of air combat and carry them back to share with their squadronmates. Those who do the job best have an opportunity to be selected for one of the flying Navy's most coveted berths—that of Top Gun's thirty-two instructors.

These men are accomplished pilots by any standard. It is virtually unheard of for a Top Gun instructor to be defeated by a student on the first three missions, and some exceptional "supersticks" on the faculty have never been bested during their entire three or four years at Miramar.

When a fleet pilot first comes up against men widely regarded by unbiased observers as some of the best ACM fliers anywhere, the match-up is like one between good high-school athletes and a band of world champions. "I flew nothing but ACM for four years," a Top Gun instructor once explained, "a couple of hops a day, three or four engagements a hop. We had all our moves down to the nth degree." The Tomcat pilot flying from a carrier, he continued, "has to fit

Closing at a combined speed of more than 1,000 mph, an F-14 *(below, left)* and an A-4 of the Top Gun aggressor force are about to streak by each other, the point in a dogfight called the pass. Though the A-4 appears to threaten the F-14, it is too close and moving too fast for even a quick shot with the cannon. This encounter will evolve into a turning contest, with each pilot attempting to maneuver for an attack against the other.

ACM in with a lot of other missions, and when he does fight, it's likely to be another Tomcat. He's making mistakes. One day he wins, next day he loses. He comes to Top Gun and he's on another planet. Be twenty-five knots off on your airspeed, be inefficient on your reversals, lose sight of that teeny little F-5 for a split second, and you're going to be dead."

The initial objective of the school is to teach the pilot to take full advantage of the airplane's capabilities without slipping beyond them. In the old days, the great fear of exceeding this so-called flight envelope was structural failure, but in modern jet fighters that danger is slight. The larger peril is the "departure," where the pilot inadvertently sends his plane outside its flight envelope into aerodynamic circumstances in which the craft becomes uncontrollable.

The precise nature of a departure depends on the flight charac-

teristics of an aircraft. The F-4 Phantom, for example, could be treacherous if the pilot pitched the plane's nose up too steeply, as he might be tempted to do if he became engaged in a dogfight. In this attitude, air can stop flowing across the wings, causing a loss of lift, and into the engine, resulting in a flame-out. Then, the Phantom can flip onto its back and enter an inverted flat spin that inevitably leads to a crash.

Though less inclined to do so than the F-4, the F-14 Tomcat can also fall into a spin from which recovery is impossible. Only the newest fly-by-wire, computer-controlled fighters such as the American F-16 and F/A-18 and the French Mirage 2000 are immune to this danger. Diagnostic computer software built into their control systems is the secret. A pilot who suddenly finds himself outside the envelope need only let go of the stick, and his electronic genie will return him to stable flight.

The Top Gun syllabus calls for 112 hours of ground school and thirty-nine flights, each involving three or four engagements. The students start out with nine missions of one fighter against one fighter. The next fifteen sorties are devoted to two against two and two versus many. The last fifteen flights concentrate on many (up to eight) against many (up to twenty)—the typical, bogey-rich "furball," as U.S. pilots call it.

A Top Gun pilot once described one against one as "a knife fight in a phone booth—mean, tough, and quick, with no room for mistakes." Mastery of the technique is essential, since every battle, no matter how complex, is no more than a collection of such duels. "In a sense, it's all 1 v. 1 up there," said a Top Gun instructor. "If you're converging on a guy in a furball, you're 1 v. 1 with him. If somebody taxies in on your eight o'clock and squeezes off a missile, you're suddenly 1 v. 1 with that missile. Evade that threat and you're going to find yourself 1 v. 1 with your bad guy again when he closes for a gun attack. If you really, really learn to fight 1 v. 1, you'll develop the skill and confidence in the airplane to survive and prevail in the multi-bogey engagements."

Unlike the Air Force's Red Flag exercises, the rules of engagement at Top Gun permit head-on passes and, in fact, many fights start that way. For safety, the instructor in an F-16 and the student in an F-14 or F/A-18 fly at slightly different altitudes until they sight each other. Or they may fly to the ACM range together and then slide apart about a mile.

When the instructor is sure that each pilot has seen the other, he radios: "Fight's on!" If neither aircraft is shot down as they race toward each other at more than 1,000 knots, then the contest becomes one of being first to keep the nose of his aircraft pointed at the opponent long enough to get off a shot. As they pass each other, both pilots turn hard. The F-14's wings, previously pinned back for speed, sweep forward automatically for maximum maneuverability as the Tomcat slows in the turn. Both aircraft weave and dodge, climb and dive, each attempting to line up for a missile or cannon shot while evading the other's aim. Often simple maneuvers win such encounters. Highly complex airshow stunts are too elaborate, too difficult to learn, and most important, too rarely applicable in combat. So students and instructors alike rely on the basics (pages 54-67).

As at Red Flag, there is little point in rubbing students' noses in their shortcomings. In some stages of the training, Top Gun instructors often coach their charges by radio. On a day when the lesson is how to avoid being gunned down from behind, an instructor lining up for a cannon attack might transmit "Approaching, guns," to make certain that his victim is aware of his presence. As he begins to track the student for a shot, he might say "Pipper on," announcing that the aiming dot of the gunsight is on the target. In a real fight, he would now be firing. Then if the student breaks out of the stream of cannon shells, the instructor might say "Pipper off. Good defensive maneuver."

Teamwork takes center stage when the students advance from one-on-one engagements to missions involving more aircraft. In this superstress, task-saturated environment, a well-coordinated two-man Tomcat crew should have a decisive advantage over the opposition flying single-seat F-16s. At long range, before a target can be seen, a RIO sitting in the backseat not only operates the radar but can actually "light off" the long-range AIM-54 Phoenix and medium-range AIM-7 Sparrow radar-guided missiles while the pilot concerns himself with flying the plane.

The AIM-9 Sidewinder and guns, which are generally used against maneuvering targets at short ranges, are under the pilot's control exclusively. Only he is in a position to coordinate the movements of his fighter with the firing of weapons in close quarters. Even so, the RIO is far from superfluous. A second set of expert eyeballs in the backseat can keep that all-important lookout to the rear and tell the pilot what type of aircraft is back there, and whether it is moving away or coming in on them. The RIO can tell his teammate how to maneuver to avoid being tagged from behind. This judgment has to be made in a split second, so the RIO has to know almost as much about aircraft performance and air-to-air combat tactics as his frontseater.

By about two-thirds of the way through the course, Top Gun students begin to show marked improvement. They know their planes as they never did before. Their bodies have responded to

131

the physical stress of daily dogfighting. G-tolerance may rise from five Gs to eight Gs before grayout sets in, and no longer do their neck and back muscles ache from the strain of twisting and turning their heads to spot the instructor sliding in behind them. They know their moves and can be more aggressive. "You bounce a guy and he pulls a sharp defensive maneuver; then all of a sudden he's offensive," said one Top Gun instructor. "Two weeks ago he didn't know how to do that."

The instructor had seen the modern manifestation of something that Manfred von Richthofen, Germany's renowned Red Baron, observed during the First World War. "It's not the crate," he said, "but the man who flies it." This maxim is as true now as it was then. Although aircraft and weapons may continue to improve dramatically, an essential ingredient of success remains the pilot himself. In the air-to-air arena, "only the spirit of attack born of a brave heart," said Adolf Galland, distinguished ace of the Third Reich, "will bring success to any fighter aircraft, no matter how highly developed it may be."

There is something else. Students at Top Gun learn one of air combat's most important concepts, albeit an unwritten one. "Lie, cheat, and steal in the cockpit," is one observer's rendition. "Leave chivalry hanging in the closet with your dress whites"—just as Joe "Hoser" Satrapa did one day in his Tomcat when he took on a Navy aggressor flying an F-5 Tiger.

Hoser Satrapa had cut his teeth in Vietnam flying the F-8 Crusader with its quartet of 20-mm cannon. He was a fiend for guns—a vocal one, too. People remember Hoser shouting at the top of his lungs: "No kill like a guns kill!"

So it was clear where Hoser stood on the subject that day when he paired off against the F-5. As the two jets lined up for takeoff in this often-told tale, Hoser used his fists to pantomime the cocking of machine guns on a World War I biplane. The other pilot gave a thumbs up. Guns it would be.

In the ACM area, both fighters set up twenty miles apart for a head-on intercept. They were seven miles from the merge and closing at more than 1,000 miles an hour when Hoser suddenly called out "Fox One"—a Sparrow missile away for a clean kill. As they met and raced past, the bewildered F-5 pilot radioed. "What the hell was that all about?" "Sorry," replied Hoser, all contrition. "Just lost my head. Let's set up again. Guns only."

With models (an A-4 Skyhawk in his right hand and an F/A-18 Hornet in his left), a Top Gun instructor makes a point to visiting Marine aviators after a training flight. Such after-action assessments play an important role in helping pilots to improve their skills—and ultimately their chance of prevailing in combat.

As the two fighter planes came at each other a second time, Hoser once again keyed his microphone at a range of seven miles. "Fox One," he called softly.

The Tomcat pilot landed first and was enjoying himself at the Officers' Club bar when the F-5 pilot stamped in, irritated at having been shot down twice in the same morning—by a student. "Hoser," he roared, "where's your credibility?"

Said Hoser, grinning: "Credibility down. Kill ratio up!" ★

Electronic Arbiters for Aerial Duels

An RTO observes an aerial engagement at his console. In front of him are two 4½-by-5-foot color monitors for enlarging the images on the computer screens. From this vantage point, the RTO can follow the movements of thirty-six aircraft in every particular while keeping tabs on the locations of up to 100 more.

As aircraft engage in mock combat above a range equipped with the Air Combat Maneuvering Instrumentation (ACMI) system *(pages 114-115)*, information from the data pods mounted on the planes pours into the nerve center on the ground. There it is monitored by a range training officer, or RTO, a rotating position assigned to various pilots from contending squadrons.

Surrounded by computer screens that enable him to follow the engagement from virtually any perspective *(left)*, the RTO referees the encounter between the two teams of fighter planes—initiating the action, observing their maneuvers, checking to see when and what type of ordnance is being fired, and noting hits. If one of the contenders "downs" another, the RTO calls out the result by radio, and the defeated pilot disengages. Back on the ground after the exercise, the pilots watch recorded replays of the action to review and critique their performances.

Pictures on the facing page show how the RTO is able to visualize the action by watching his computer screens. The four pages that follow depict an actual air combat training mission as viewed by an RTO at Homestead Air Force Base, near Miami, Florida. A team of F-16s *(red on the computer screens)* has been assigned the mission of attacking a submerged wreck just over 100 miles away. An opposing team of F-4s *(blue)* attempts to defend the target, engaging the Red Air Team in a dogfight. In this exercise, the RTO tracks the aerial battle from the standpoint of the Red Air Team's aircraft 5, as the pilot engages aircraft 13 and 14 of the defending Blue Air Team.

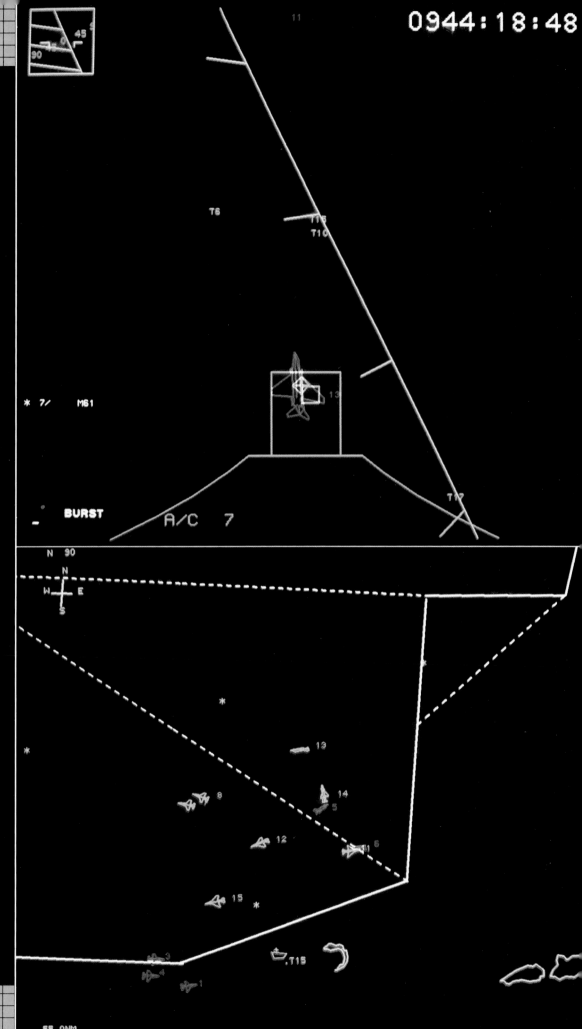

The cockpit view from Blue Air Team's aircraft 7 conveys a wealth of data to the RTO. The diagonal horizon line shows the plane has banked sharply to the left, an attitude echoed in the box in the upper left corner. By turning, the pilot holds a small blue box and a diamond of similar size—used together in the F-16 for aiming heat-seeking Sidewinder missiles—on the enemy target: Red Team's aircraft 13. Red 11, too distant for the pilot of Blue 7 to see, appears without an aircraft symbol at the top of the screen next to the time, which is reported to the hundredth of a second. A yellow number accompanied by a *T* denotes a landmark on the ground.

The monitor can portray a comprehensive overview of the action, known to pilots as a god's-eye view. The scale can be adjusted; in this case the image on the screen spans fifty-five nautical miles. Aircraft of the Blue and Red teams are numbered for identification, while T15 denotes the submerged ship. Although it lies outside normal range boundaries *(solid white lines)*, it can still be monitored by the ACMI system. Dotted lines mark alternative boundaries that require special activation. The shape to the right of the ship is an island in the Marquesas; farther to the right appear the westernmost of the Florida Keys.

1456:20:32

✈ 14

A/C   5

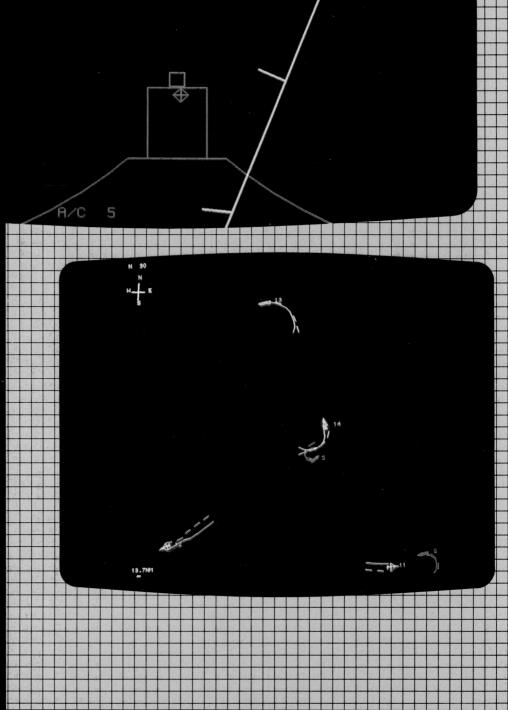

"Fight's on!" With these words, the RTO initiates the air battle. Seconds later, the cockpit view *(above)* shows Red aircraft 5 banking sharply to the left in an effort to gain an infrared-missile lock on Blue 14, which turns to escape. That the fighter appears to be turning right is a result of the red plane having rolled nearly onto its back. In the god's-eye view *(right),* solid and dotted lines trailing from the contending aircraft are called history trails. They show where the planes have been for the past several seconds and help clarify maneuvers. The trails indicate that Red 5 has rolled into a sharp turn as he closes on Blue 14, which is turning left to avoid its assailant. The pilot of Blue 13 is turning to come to the aid of his wingman, while in the lower right-hand corner another dogfight is shaping up between Blue 11 and Red 6.

1456:24:52

13

14

A/C 5

N 90
N
W—E
S

13

14

5

13.7XX 12

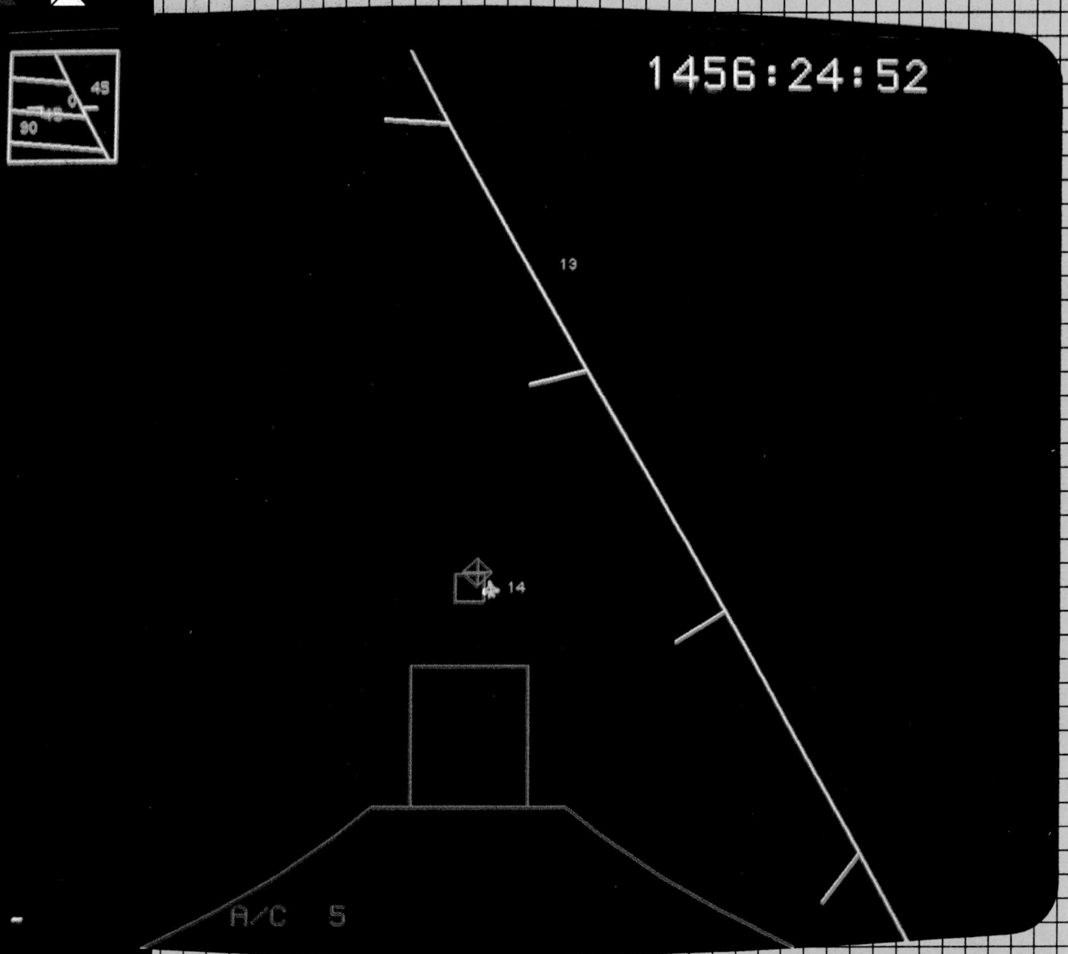

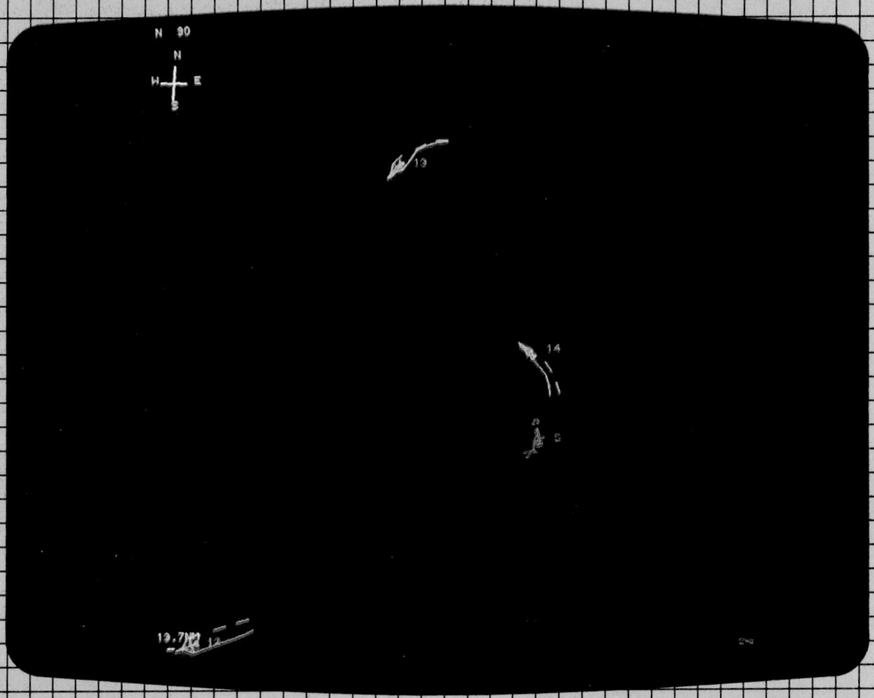

Little more than four seconds into the battle, Red 5 is in a good position to fire a missile at Blue 14. The blue number 13 in the cockpit view pinpoints Blue 14's flight leader for the RTO, but the absence of an aircraft symbol indicates that this plane is too far away for the pilot of Red 5 to see. The god's-eye monitor shows Red 5 locking his Sidewinder's heat seeker onto Blue 14, as indicated by the wedge-shaped line in front of the red jet's nose. Blue 13 continues his turn to the aid of his wingman, while Blue 12 *(lower left)* is about to move offscreen to join his leader, Blue 11.

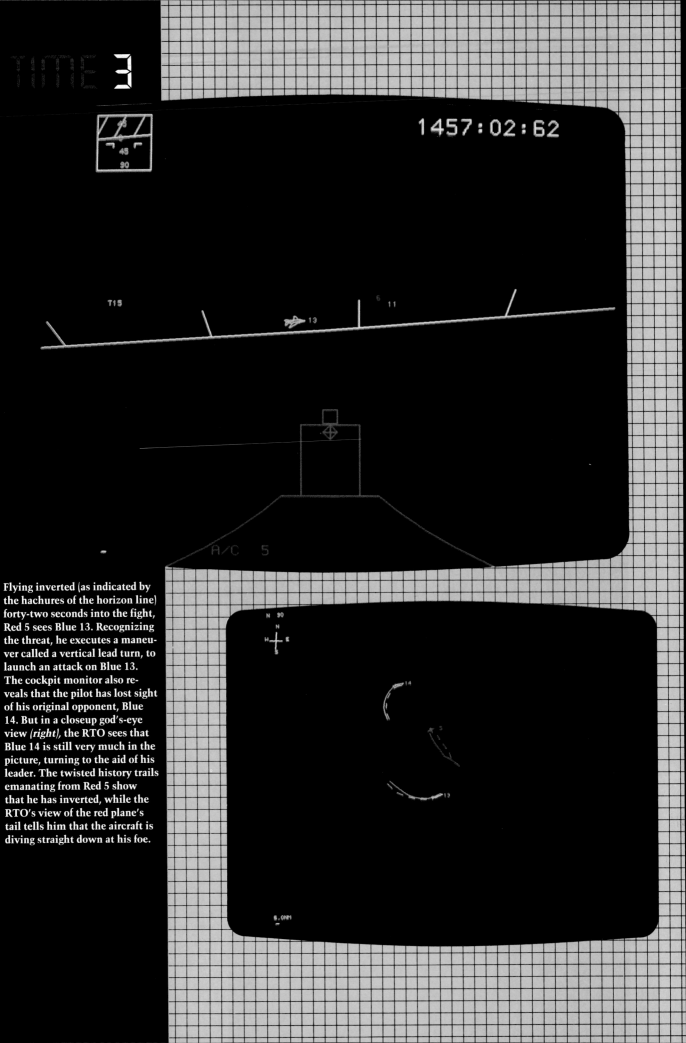

TIME 3

1457:02:62

A/C 5

Flying inverted (as indicated by the hachures of the horizon line) forty-two seconds into the fight, Red 5 sees Blue 13. Recognizing the threat, he executes a maneuver called a vertical lead turn, to launch an attack on Blue 13. The cockpit monitor also reveals that the pilot has lost sight of his original opponent, Blue 14. But in a closeup god's-eye view *(right)*, the RTO sees that Blue 14 is still very much in the picture, turning to the aid of his leader. The twisted history trails emanating from Red 5 show that he has inverted, while the RTO's view of the red plane's tail tells him that the aircraft is diving straight down at his foe.

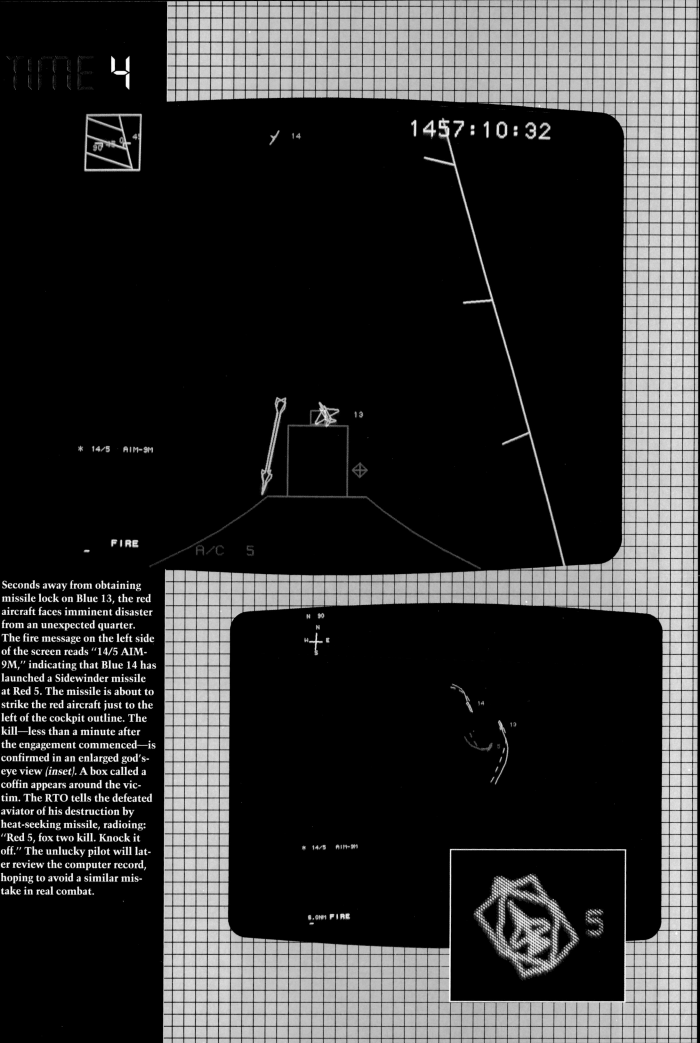

1457:10:32

14

13

* 14/5 AIM-9M

FIRE

A/C 5

N 90
N
W   E
S

14

13

5

* 14/5 AIM-9M

8.0NM FIRE

S

Seconds away from obtaining missile lock on Blue 13, the red aircraft faces imminent disaster from an unexpected quarter. The fire message on the left side of the screen reads "14/5 AIM-9M," indicating that Blue 14 has launched a Sidewinder missile at Red 5. The missile is about to strike the red aircraft just to the left of the cockpit outline. The kill—less than a minute after the engagement commenced—is confirmed in an enlarged god's-eye view *(inset)*. A box called a coffin appears around the victim. The RTO tells the defeated aviator of his destruction by heat-seeking missile, radioing: "Red 5, fox two kill. Knock it off." The unlucky pilot will later review the computer record, hoping to avoid a similar mistake in real combat.

Bold Designs for Superfighters

The stealthy shapes that characterize the Northrop-McDonnell Douglas candidate for the next-generation U.S. fighter are evident in this photo of the YF-23 on its maiden flight on August 27, 1990. The wings and canted tail surfaces have a radar-evading configuration: triangles tapering to squared-off tips. Wing blends smoothly into fuselage, eliminating sharp angles, and the twin engine nozzles are recessed forward to mask them from heat-seeking missiles.

It was not a fast aircraft, nor was it sleek and racy-looking, like most fighters. But air superiority was not what British designers had in mind in 1967 when the first British Aerospace Harrier took to the skies; their ungainly creation was meant for reconnaissance, ground attack, and close troop support under battlefield conditions directly behind the front lines. And in seeking to achieve that capability, the designers had endowed the Harrier with an innovation termed "vectored thrust"—a remarkable set of engine nozzles that could be rotated forward, enabling the Harrier to hover on its deflected jet blast, and thus land and take off on a postage stamp, without benefit of runway.

Now, in the spring of 1975, a Harrier in U.S. Marine Corps livery and bearing the American designation AV-8A was about to make air combat history—whether it was meant to or not.

As a diversion, Major Del Weber and his mates in Attack Squad-

The United States and the Soviet Union are not likely to be the only nations flying advanced tactical fighters in the 1990s. In Europe, aeronautical engineers are working on a trio of formidable aircraft to vie for technological supremacy in the years ahead.

Of roughly similar design, the French Rafale, the Eurofighter from a four-nation consortium, and the Swedish JAS-39 Gripen are single-seat fighters engineered for both mach 2 speed (1,320 mph) and supermaneuverability. All employ a geometry that marries a delta wing to moving canards; this design offers exceptional agility, but because it is inherently unstable, the three air-

RAFALE

ron VMA-513 based in the Philippines had been practicing some interesting air-to-air maneuvers using the Harrier's vectored-thrust engine. A few thoughtful naval air tacticians had heard about the experiments and had set up a dogfight against an F-14 from the carrier *Enterprise:* the big, supersonic Tomcat versus the subsonic, ground-hugging Harrier.

"Nightmare Two-Six, I've got you in sight," came the voice of the Tomcat pilot. "I'm at your three." Climbing to 12,000 feet, Del Weber acknowledged his call sign and banked toward the F-14. Seconds later the two planes were flying abeam, 4,000 feet apart. With a signal, each turned into the other for a head-on pass. Weber watched the Tomcat blast by at 350 knots, its fully extended wings indicating the pilot's intention of keeping the fight in close. The combatants reversed into opposing circles, each chasing the other's tail. The fight was on.

It should have been no contest—so long as the Tomcat could dictate the battle, with its speed and long-range missiles. But this was to be a close-in dogfight. The speeds would be fairly even to start with, and Weber would do all he could to force the Tomcat to fly within the Harrier's performance envelope.

For what seemed like an eternity the two planes twisted and racked about the sky, jockeying for advantage. Finally, the Tomcat

craft will rely on computerized fly-by-wire controls like those used on the U.S. F-16.

Though less stealthy than the U.S. YF-23, the European designs nevertheless incorporate blended surfaces and energy-absorptive composite materials for smaller radar cross sections; the Rafale, for example, has a radar signature less than two-thirds that of the F-16. The three fighters will also feature the latest avionics equipment. Ease of maintenance and short turnaround times are critical factors in the designs. The three aircraft will play both ground-attack and air-superiority roles. And the Gripen can be configured for reconnaissance simply by switching computer software.

JAS-39 GRIPEN

The Rafale and the Gripen are already in flight test, with deliveries scheduled to start in the mid-1990s. The Eurofighter—a joint enterprise including Britain, Germany, Italy, and Spain—is expected to fly in late 1991 and enter air force inventories in 1996. All told, six European air forces would like to buy nearly 1,500 of the fighters.

EUROFIGHTER

and the Harrier were locked in a rolling scissors where, like a large corkscrew, each pilot attempted to roll behind the other and get into firing position.

The speed was down below 250 knots, and the F-14 was in the world of the Harrier. The Tomcat was approaching the low end of its envelope, but the Harrier was perfectly at home. "I waited until I was on top, inverted, as the bandit was pulling through the bottom fighting gravity," recalled Weber. "As he started to pitch back for his next roll I gained a big advantage at a critical time. I cranked in about thirty-five degrees of nozzle, causing my aircraft to finally close the angle by using the Harrier's thrust vectoring capabilities."

By rotating his thrust toward the horizontal while rolling inverted, Weber had made the Harrier literally drop down on the Tomcat. "I almost had him but he managed to stay just out of my sights," said Weber. Now the two fighters wrenched into another scissors,

143

crossed at ninety degrees, and Weber maneuvered swiftly to realign with the Tomcat. "It was time to put on the heat," said the Marine pilot. "As my nose passed through a vertical position, pointing toward the Tomcat below, a time where other airplanes would gain excess speed and overshoot, I slammed the nozzles to full reverse thrust." The nozzles rotated forward until they were almost twenty degrees beyond hover position—and the Harrier maintained a constant 200 knots of airspeed even though it was nose down and in a diving turn on the target.

The range was now less than 1,500 feet and the Tomcat was cooked. "All through this maneuver I easily stayed inside the Tomcat's turn to maintain a gun attack," related Weber. "I watched as my aimdot neared his airplane, then passed through its canopy." But before Weber could call the shot, the F-14's pilot saw that he had been trapped. He keyed his mike and called "Blazer"—meaning "You got me."

No fewer than twenty-five other engagements were flown that day—and in twenty-three of them the Harriers of VMA-513 were victorious, in large measure because of the amazing maneuvers made possible by "VIFFing" (Vectoring in Forward Flight). No other aircraft of the 1970s had that capability; nor did any of the 1980s fighters, all of which were developed in the mid-1970s. But the designers of future aircraft—the fighters of the 1990s and beyond—would take careful note. And vectored thrust—with its contribution to supermaneuverability—would be among the many stunning advances that would take tomorrow's fighter pilots to the edges of manned aerial combat.

The Next Generation: How Nimble, How Swift

A jet fighter without the agility to grapple with a darting foe or to elude an attack is all but useless in an air-superiority role. The nimbleness required of such aircraft comes primarily from two sources: power and aerodynamics. The stronger the engine of a fighter, the more quickly it can gain momentum for the first thrust in a dogfight, regain it after a series of energy-draining maneuvers, or accelerate out of the encounter should the odds become unfavorable. Equally important is the

Taking off on its maiden flight on September 29, 1990, the YF-22 advanced tactical fighter prototype exhibits exhaust nozzles that will give it a measure of vectored thrust. The design team led by Lockheed has incorporated scalloped movable nozzles that will deflect engine thrust through a range of twenty degrees up or down, thus permitting much-enhanced combat maneuvers.

ability of wings and tail to cause abrupt changes in the aircraft's direction of flight.

Yet neither goal is independent of the other. As Major Del Weber showed with his Harrier, rethinking the application of thrust can increase an engine's contribution in an area traditionally left to aerodynamics. And advances in airframes can make an engine seem more powerful; a sleek aircraft reduces the air resistance called drag, and a light one accelerates more quickly than a heavy one.

Virtually every major military power, recognizing that falling behind in the air-superiority arena could cause defeat in some future conflict, has a new fighter under development. In the autumn of 1990, the United States unveiled a pair of advanced tactical fighter (ATF) prototypes that embody every state-of-the-art technology from vectored-thrust engines that permit supersonic speed without lighting the afterburner ("supercruise") to so-called stealth technology for a low radar profile. Lockheed, Boeing, and General Dynamics have teamed up to build the YF-22, while Northrop and McDonnell Douglas are paired on the YF-23. In Europe, a consortium including Britain, Germany, Italy, and Spain is developing the Eurofighter; France's Dassault, producer of the famed Mirage series, is betting on its Rafale; Sweden has the new Saab Gripen; and the Soviets are known to be developing at least two advanced air-combat designs.

Although these fighters are less than revolutionary, they are all very expensive. American advanced tactical fighters are expected to cost $50 million per copy, approximately twice the price of the F-15 Eagle. With the Air Force and Navy together wishing to purchase 1,250 aircraft, the outlay could be a staggering $64 billion. At such prices, the world's air forces may have to refit current fighters with new wings and more powerful engines. Candidates in the United States are the Eagle, the F/A-18 Hornet, and the F-16 Falcon. Else-

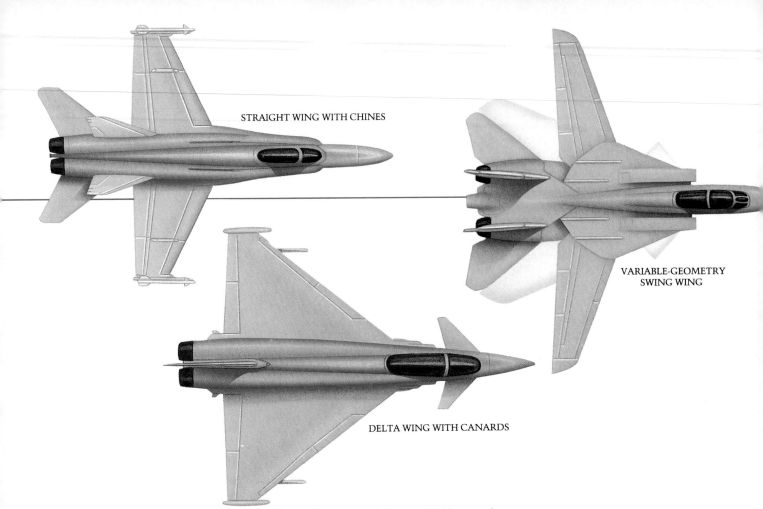

STRAIGHT WING WITH CHINES

VARIABLE-GEOMETRY
SWING WING

DELTA WING WITH CANARDS

where, Europe's Panavia Tornado and France's Mirage 2000 may be rehabilitated in this fashion, as might the Soviet MiG-29 Fulcrum and the Su-27 Flanker.

Nevertheless, most authorities regard upgrading of aircraft designed during the 1970s as a stopgap measure. Every airframe eventually reaches the end of its service life, and someday, new fighters like the ATFs will enter the world's inventory.

Aerodynamic inventiveness is nowhere more evident than in the wings. One innovation of the 1960s, for example, was the swing wing, which extends for slow maneuvering and sweeps back for speed. Although adopted for the Navy's F-14 Tomcat and other aircraft, variable-geometry wings have shortcomings. For example, the mechanism for moving the wing contains heavy motors, gears, and pivots. Discarding them would allow greater fuel capacity or payload. Furthermore, swing-wing aircraft loom large on radar because of beam-reflecting corners and edges.

For these reasons, the swing wing is absent from the plans for all the new fighters. American ATF prototypes have fixed wings with rear, or trailing, edges that slant forward to a squared tip almost as sharply as the leading edge sweeps back *(page 140)*. This wing shape concentrates stress near the fuselage, where the wings are the strongest. By some estimates, the design enables the aircraft to pull twelve Gs in a turn, three more than the most nimble current-generation fighters.

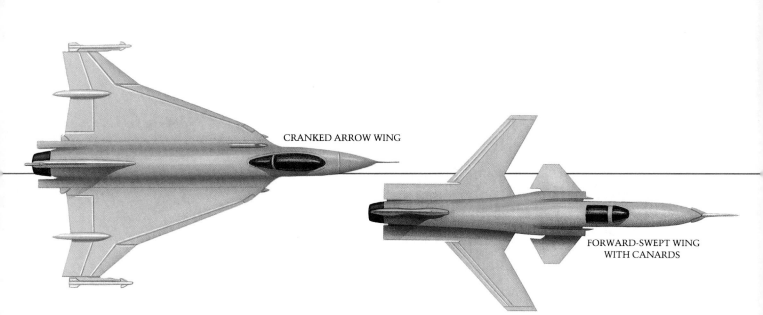

CRANKED ARROW WING

FORWARD-SWEPT WING
WITH CANARDS

Although the perfect wing has yet to be designed, aeronautical engineers have performed marvels of innovation in their never-ending pursuit of speed and agility. Some wing shapes are illustrated above. The conventional straight wing excels at high-speed intercepts and maneuverability, especially when teamed with chines (thin lifting strips situated at the junction of wing and fuselage). The variable-geometry form permits takeoffs from short runways as well as mach 2-plus flight when the wings are swept back. The delta shape, teamed with canards, and the cranked arrow offer superior handling through all speed ranges, while supporting uncommonly heavy payloads. And the experimental forward-swept wing has shown an unrivaled nimbleness that is ideal for close-quarter combat.

Advanced fighters of other nations hold to the triangular delta wing, long known to reduce drag and provide superior handling at both high and low speeds compared with the simple, swept-back wing that preceded it. To enhance the delta wing's agility, European and Soviet designers have positioned small winglets near the cockpit. Called canards, these appendages were pioneered on modern fighters by the Swedish Viggen and the Israeli Kfir. The winglets increase lift and reduce stress on the main wings. By redirecting airflow across the wings, canards in effect decrease the angle of attack (the angle between the wing and the wind streaming across it) when a pilot pulls the control stick toward himself to climb or to hold a turn. Angle of attack is a limiting factor in aircraft performance; a pilot exceeding the maximum for his aircraft will experience a stall, in which air begins to flow turbulently over the wing, destroying lift and often causing loss of control.

A promising variation of the canard is being flight-tested on a modified F-16 Falcon. Known as the F-16AT, this aircraft carries a pair of foreplanes angled downward from the engine air intake. Governed by computer, these foreplanes act like front-mounted rudders, enabling the pilot to slue the airplane without banking. In the wink of an eye, a flier could whip his aircraft into firing position against an enemy forty degrees or even fifty degrees off his nose.

A second experimental F-16, known as the F-16XL, employs a "cranked arrow" wing design. It begins at the cockpit with fifty degrees of sweep, then juts out at a thirty-degree angle toward the tips. The wing doubles the 300-square-foot wing area of the standard Falcon, adding fuel capacity, improving fuel efficiency at cruising speed, and increasing payload.

Whatever the shape of the wing, however, its aluminum skin, fastened by rivets, is fading into aeronautical history. Instead, space-age materials—aluminum-lithium, boron, Kevlar, as well as

fibers of aramid, carbon, and glass—constitute between 40 percent and 60 percent by weight of the YF-23 and YF-22. Bonded together with adhesives stronger than rivets, these materials are much more expensive than aluminum. But they are lighter and stronger, and they are generally poor reflectors of radar.

Power can also help thwart an attack, though more through the acceleration it makes possible than with top speed. No one discounts the need to get to a battle quickly, but after opposing forces merge, airspeeds drop dramatically. Most dogfights take place between 250 mph and about 800 mph, and within this range, it is the zip derived from a high thrust-to-weight ratio that counts.

Heretofore, this spurt of power came from afterburners, devices that spray fuel into the exhaust on its way out the tailpipe. After-burners can double thrust, but in doing so, they can also quadruple fuel consumption. An F-15 in afterburner empties its tanks at the astonishing rate of 2,500 pounds per minute, quickly enough to deplete its entire fuel load in less than seven minutes.

Power plants for twenty-first-century fighters, though not abandoning the afterburner, will reduce its contribution in air-to-air engagements. At full throttle without afterburner, these engines will produce as much thrust as today's power plants generate with

An X-29 experimental aircraft dances through the sky with its nose raised fifty degrees above its flight path *(contrail)*, **ten to twenty degrees higher than other fighters. This exceptional agility is made possible by the X-29's forward-swept wing. The subject of experiments by the Germans in World War II, such a wing was impractical until the invention of new materials strong enough to withstand the huge stresses imposed by the design.**

the afterburner lit—and do so with 40 percent fewer parts and considerably improved fuel efficiency.

In the ATFs, such engines will produce 2.2 pounds of thrust for every pound of aircraft weight, allowing the fighters to accelerate up to 40 percent faster than the F-16 Falcon, which boasts only a 1.6-to-1 thrust-to-weight ratio. The difference could be the decisive margin in combat.

Top speeds will not increase noticeably. Flat out in afterburner, the ATFs will retain the mach 2.5-plus dash capability of current F-15s, a speed deemed sufficient by Air Force tacticians. Although all modern air-superiority fighters can exceed mach 1, they all require such a fuel-devouring boost from afterburners that only the briefest supersonic dashes are practical. The new engines, however, can supply the necessary thrust without resorting to afterburners.

A number of the advanced fighters will go a step further by embracing vectored thrust. In the case of the YF-22, vanes to deflect engine exhaust are attached to the engine tailpipes instead of being installed amidships as they are in the Harrier. With this arrangement, the YF-22 will be able to operate from a runway only 1,500 feet long (an F-15 needs 3,500 feet), and the pilot, by changing the angle of the deflectors, can pitch the nose up or down much more rapidly than he can with control surfaces alone.

For steering, the ATFs will dispense with the weighty, and vulnerable, hydraulic systems that have been in use since the 1950s. Instead, they will incorporate technology known as fly-by-wire (FBW), which had its military debut in the late 1970s on the F-16 Falcon. As the name suggests, the system depends on electronic signals rather than hydraulic fluid to translate a pilot's movements of the controls into action. When the pilot presses on the stick or rudder pedals, a computer measures how much to move the appropriate surfaces and signals actuators to do so.

An FBW system is lighter and easier to maintain than a hydraulic system and, being quadruply redundant, stands to be less susceptible to battle damage. But like all electronics, there is no such thing as a slow leak; either a component works or it does not. Moreover, fly-by-wire technology is subject to electrical interference—from a nuclear airburst, perhaps, or a massive jamming effort. Even in peacetime, F-16 pilots in Europe have had control problems after flying near powerful radio transmitters.

Some of these flaws will disappear in a newer system that incorporates fiberoptic cables in place of wires. In fly-by-light (FBL), strands of glass carry pulses of laser light that trigger control actuators, much as electronic signals do. The FBL cables are immune to interference and are extremely light in weight. But fiberoptic systems are expensive, and they demand specialized training for maintenance personnel. Still, the advantages of fly-by-light so far outweigh those of fly-by-wire that they are the controls of choice for the American twenty-first-century fighter.

Arming the Superfighters

A pilot flying the next generation of air-superiority fighters will have the same three settings for the weapons-management system aboard his aircraft that have been there for more than thirty years: one position for guns and the others for two types of missiles—radar-homing and heat-seeking. And while new air-to-air weapons sparkle in the eyes of inventors and engineers—one proposal envisions accelerating projectiles by means of powerful magnetic fields instead of explosives—they are unlikely to arm any new fighter for several decades. In the meantime, the teeth bared in a dogfight will have a familiar gleam.

The cannon going into the YF-22 and YF-23 is the venerable M-61 Vulcan—six 20-mm barrels that rotate Gatling-gun-style to spew out 6,000 explosive shells per minute, so fast that it will empty the magazine of either ATF in less than ten seconds. No aircraft can survive the Vulcan's storm; in a demonstration filmed not long after the gun's introduction in 1958, the tail assembly of a drone helicopter target simply disappeared, almost as if bitten off by an invisible presence.

In Vietnam, pilots scoring against enemy fighters with the Vulcan fired bursts lasting about three seconds, on average. Thus, the M-61 can be expected to run out of ammunition after only two or three passes. Even so, the Air Force wants a quicker-shooting model, perhaps with a larger bore. In an age of aircraft equipped with vectored-thrust engines, movable canards, or other features that improve the ability of fighters to dodge bullets, a pilot may be unable to track a target long enough for a lethal burst unless the gun can fire at least 8,000 heavier, more destructive rounds per minute.

The heat-seeking missile is the deadly AIM-9 Sidewinder. (AIM stands for air-intercept missile.) Even older than the Vulcan, the Sidewinder is in its thirteenth incarnation. Over the years, its infrared guidance system has been improved so that it can home on a fighter's exhaust plume from any angle, not just from the rear. Because it ignores temperatures hotter than those of jet-engine emissions, the latest model is much less likely than earlier ones to be decoyed by flares launched from an evading aircraft. The warhead has doubled in weight to 22.5 pounds of high explosive that propels a lethal spray of metal fragments. A clever proximity fuse uses a small Doppler radar to sense a target within this sphere and detonate the warhead—but only if the rate of closure begins to decrease, an indication that the target might be eluding the missile.

To reach out beyond the Vulcan and the Sidewinder, the Air Force and the Navy plan to replace the old—and somewhat unreliable—AIM-7 Sparrow radar-homing missile with the AIM-120 AMRAAM (advanced medium range air-to-air missile). Equipped with a long-burning, powerful rocket motor, the AMRAAM has a range of fifty miles, twice the Sparrow's. It is also more maneuverable. Most important to pilots, however, is the AMRAAM's ability to find its own way to the target, independently of the fighter's radar. This launch-and-leave capability permits the pilot to fire a missile at a second target—or begin evasive action—before the first missile reaches its mark. In less threatening situations, control of the missile can be made to alternate between the AMRAAM's own radar and the fighter's, a tactic intended to defeat an enemy's electronic countermeasures.

Like the Sparrow, the Navy's AIM-54 Phoenix is scheduled for retirement. Carried on F-14 Tomcats, the Phoenix, with a range in excess of ninety miles, was designed in the 1960s to protect aircraft carriers by knocking down attacking planes before they could get close enough to launch missiles against the ship. Now that air-launched cruise missiles have ranges greater than 100 miles, the Phoenix has become outmoded. Its replacement will be a version of a weapon called the AAAM (advanced air-to-air missile).

Engineers expect additional range for the AAAM to come from a ramjet engine. Burning ordinary jet fuel, a ramjet is the simplest of all jet engines and a model of efficiency compared to a rocket motor. Built with no moving parts, a ramjet forces air into the engine by virtue of speed alone instead of relying on a spinning compressor

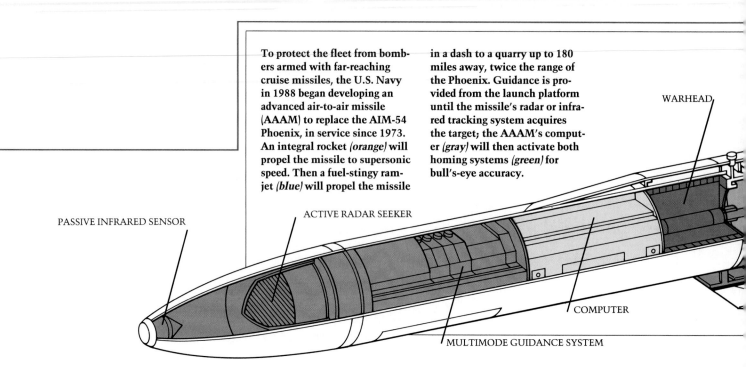

To protect the fleet from bombers armed with far-reaching cruise missiles, the U.S. Navy in 1988 began developing an advanced air-to-air missile (AAAM) to replace the AIM-54 Phoenix, in service since 1973. An integral rocket *(orange)* will propel the missile to supersonic speed. Then a fuel-stingy ramjet *(blue)* will propel the missile in a dash to a quarry up to 180 miles away, twice the range of the Phoenix. Guidance is provided from the launch platform until the missile's radar or infrared tracking system acquires the target; the AAAM's computer *(gray)* will then activate both homing systems *(green)* for bull's-eye accuracy.

PASSIVE INFRARED SENSOR

ACTIVE RADAR SEEKER

WARHEAD

COMPUTER

MULTIMODE GUIDANCE SYSTEM

like that in a turbojet. The faster a ramjet travels, the better it works. However, it does not function at all moving at speeds much less than 500 mph. For acceleration to this velocity, the AAAM will depend on a small rocket booster.

In addition to a hybrid propulsion system, the AAAM is expected to have an exceedingly accurate, multimode guidance system containing both an infrared detector and a radar-guidance system that can operate either passively or actively. In its passive mode, it homes on signals emitted by the target's radar. In its active mode, the system sends out its own signals. To counter any attempt by a target to deceive the guidance system as the missile approaches, the AAAM will alternate automatically between its radar- and infrared-homing modes as the missile closes for the kill.

To Fight Another Day

Advanced tactical fighter prototypes are enormous airplanes. The YF-22, for example, looked "bulky" to observers on its maiden flight in September 1990. It seemed more massive even than the F-15 Eagle chase plane, a huge aircraft with a maximum takeoff weight of 68,000 pounds, about the same as a Boeing 737 jetliner when empty. The competing YF-23 appears larger still. Almost seventy feet in length, it is four feet longer than the Eagle. Such dimensions are necessary if the new fighters are to carry the fuel, instruments, and weapons they need to do their jobs. The bigger the aircraft, however, the easier target it becomes, so the new generation will employ every trick in the book to ensure their survival.

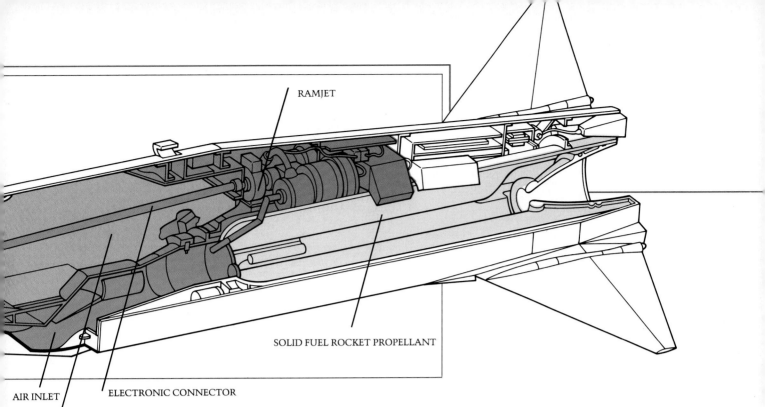

RAMJET

SOLID FUEL ROCKET PROPELLANT

AIR INLET

ELECTRONIC CONNECTOR

RAMJET LIQUID FUEL TANK

Many of the old defenses will remain in service to defeat threats from both ground and air. Flares that give off a hotter signature than jet tailpipes will be launched by computer at the most advantageous moment to counter heat-seeking missiles. Silvery clouds of chaff—short filaments of radar-reflecting material—will be dispensed to mask the aircraft and confuse radar-homing missiles. In a new twist, the chaff dispenser will act on radar-frequency data supplied by the plane's sensors, automatically cutting filaments to the optimum length to baffle whatever enemy radar may be tracking the aircraft at the moment. To reduce dependence on special-purpose electronic-warfare aircraft, which howl away at enemy radars and bedevil enemy radio communications, the new fighters—ATFs or upgrades—will carry a full suite of powerful, highly miniaturized jammers of their own.

None of these measures is infallible. Enemy radars in particular are likely to have their own tricks for seeing past such ruses. Thus it would be far better never to be detected than to rely on such uncertain allies for survival—a concept that has led to so-called stealth technology. First applied to subsonic aircraft such as the B-2 bomber and the F-117 fighter-bomber, stealth principles made their supersonic, air-superiority debut in the YF-22 and YF-23.

Aircraft make excellent radar reflectors; radar beams glint off their aluminum skins just as sunbeams do. But shapes are important as well. Strong radar reflections come from rims of engine inlets, from spinning turbine blades just inside, from right angles such as those formed between the vertical and horizontal stabilizers at the tail, and from gaps in the airframe such as those found at the joints of ailerons, rudders, flaps, and swing wings. Together, the reflectivities of these components add up to a figure called the radar

In Modern Design, Less Is More

Aircraft operating in the modern combat environment are increasingly targeted by missiles equipped with extremely accurate seekers that home on radar or thermal signatures.

The technologies emerging to thwart such smart missiles include building with nonmetallic compounds, coating with radar-absorbent materials, and upgrading electronic countermeasures. The most visible advances, though, have come by modifying an aircraft's basic shape to shrink its radar cross section, or RCS, the image it generates on a radarscope.

Objects with flat vertical surfaces and surfaces lying at right angles to each other produce the strongest radar returns. For that reason, YF-23 designers gave their new plane a noticeably different shape than the company's present-generation F-15 Eagle. Among the key areas are the tail, where the F-15's four-surface, right-angled assemblage evolved on the YF-23 into two surfaces canted at forty-five-degree angles; the underside, where missiles and fuel tank have been moved within the fuselage; and the engine intakes, which have been relocated and shaped to reduce radar returns.

The effect of minimizing radar reflectivity is extraordinary. The F-15 is visible on radar at a distance of around eighty-five miles. The YF-23 remains invisible to radar until it comes within twenty miles. In fighter pilot parlance, the difference means: "First Look. First Shot. First Kill."

cross section (RCS). The RCS of a plane is usually expressed as the area of a flat steel plate that would cause a radar reflection of equal strength. For example, a B-52 bomber has a radar cross section matching that of a plate having an area of 107 square feet.

Both the YF-22 and YF-23 employ a wide range of approaches to minimizing RCS. For example, the right angle between vertical and horizontal stabilizers is absent, these components having been replaced by a pair of angled tail fins. The throats of air intakes for the engines are shaped so that any radar waves reaching the compressor blades cannot be reflected directly back toward the radar set where they originated. Advanced tactical fighter fuselages exhibit a degree of faceting and blending. Faceting describes an assembly of flat surfaces, angled to deflect radar beams away from a radar station. Blending, in which sharp angles between adjacent surfaces are replaced by a gradual transition of one surface into the other, induces the radar beam to "flow" around the structure instead of being directly reflected.

To complement these techniques, the aluminum skins typical of fighters designed before the mid-1980s will give way to other coverings that will work to thwart detection by hostile radar. Known collectively as radar-absorbent materials, they constitute a new class of composites that contain thousands of tiny ferromagnetic "absorbers" spaced closely together throughout. Shaped in various forms—often a cross—they bounce the radar beams back and forth within the skin until the beams' energy is absorbed or otherwise dissipated.

The combined effects of these techniques are expected to be dramatic. Stealth experts estimate that with careful attention to design and construction—and accepting various trade-offs necessary in a supersonic aircraft, such as exposed air intakes for engines—an air-superiority fighter the size of the new ATFs can be made with an RCS smaller than that of a Volkswagen Beetle.

Such a target, of course, would not be totally invisible to radar, but it could fly much closer to a radar transmitter before being detected. The effect could be to tear holes in the carefully woven fabric of an air-defense system, rents that would require many additional missiles or antiaircraft artillery pieces to mend. SAM sites, for example, are positioned so that the radar coverage of each overlaps the coverage of its neighbor. This spacing, however, assumes an RCS much larger than that of a stealthy fighter, for which radar coverage would not overlap unless more sites were added to fill the gaps. In an aerial encounter with enemy fighters, a stealthy fighter has a great advantage. The builders of the YF-23 judge that, in a head-on encounter with Soviet-built Su-27s or with future, stealthier models, the ATF could fire all its long-range radar-guided missiles before it even appeared on the opposing planes' radars.

Help for the Overburdened Pilot

Quickly pushing the control stick all the way to one side, kicking in full rudder, and then pulling back on the stick to keep the nose up is the recipe for starting the tightest turn a fighter can make. This kind of maneuver, common in air-to-air combat, places the pilot under great strain. Entering such a turn, he feels his body being squashed into the seat by rapidly building G forces. At three Gs, his head and arms feel three times their normal weight. His skin sags, and his heart has difficulty pumping blood to his brain. As Gs increase, his voice becomes the grunt of a man straining to lift a great weight. Breathing becomes a struggle.

The pilot's G-suit inflates like an enormous blood-pressure cuff around his legs and abdomen to restrict the flow of blood to his lower extremities. But above six Gs, the suit no longer helps. Blood starts to drain away from the pilot's head and into his abdomen, legs, and feet. With the brain craving oxygen, colors fade toward gray, and his field of view narrows as tunnel vision sets in. In tighter turns, the progressively darker gray can turn to black oblivion—and the pilot loses consciousness. At this point, he is in mortal danger. With luck—and if his aircraft rights itself when his hands fall away from the controls—he will not be shot down, nor will his plane go out of control during the forty-five seconds that will pass before he regains his senses.

Blackout, grayout, and the lesser discomforts of air combat have been the fighter pilot's constant companions since the first high-performance aircraft entered service in World War II. But now, with planes being designed for twelve-G or even fifteen-G maneuvers, the man in the cockpit may be the weakest link in the system.

The men who fly such machines already are aerospace athletes, conditioned with special attention to G-combating musculature. A new, full-body G-suit is under development to improve the brain's blood supply in maneuvers exceeding seven Gs. Reclining the seat also helps by keeping the pilot's feet more on a plane with his head. The seat in the F-16 Falcon, for example, tilts backward at an angle of thirty degrees, and some designers envision a forty-five-degree seat. However, many aviators prefer a more erect seat, complaining that the F-16 seat limits the pilot's ability to look over his shoulder by turning his head. Heeding such objections, designers of the YF-23 prototype, for example, reclined the seat less but raised the rudder pedals four inches. This solution is not as effective as tilting the seat because it does not lower the head. It is, nonetheless, expected to stave off blackout threshold to about nine Gs. The ultimate goal is to boost pilot tolerance to twelve Gs, perhaps thirteen. Beyond that point, damage to human tissue occurs.

The struggle against the oppressive, artificial gravity of high-G maneuvering makes it all the more difficult for a fighter pilot to monitor all the warning lights, engine gauges, navigation instruments, weapons-systems indicators, radarscopes, threat detectors, radios, and switches—more than 190 devices in some older fighters—that compete for their attention. And the aerial battles of tomorrow will be fought at levels of technology that may overwhelm aviators with information. To eliminate this sensory overload, cockpits have come to filter out more and more inessential information and to display the most critical facts in ways that are instantly intelligible. Cockpits in a future generation of fighters—perhaps the one following the ATFs—will go even further in their efforts to assist the man behind the oxygen mask.

The cockpit of the F-16C Falcon is a step in that direction. Designed in the mid-1970s, it has a simplified instrument panel that makes use of two cathode-ray tubes called multifunction displays (MFDs) on either side of the cockpit. The pilot has access to a wide variety of essential information—inertial navigation, aircraft sensors, or weapons status—on these six-inch-square, TV-like screens. A set of buttons surrounds each MFD. Their function changes depending on the display the pilot has called up. This reduces the number of control switches cluttering the cockpit.

Moreover, the F-16 retains an idea pioneered in the F-15 Eagle. Both aircraft have a stick and a throttle that enable an aviator to engage in combat without removing his hands from the controls. In this kind of system—known as HOTAS, for hands-on throttle and stick—these controls are studded with more buttons to press than a human has fingers and thumbs to manipulate them. A trigger and eight buttons on the control stick allow the pilot to release bombs, fire guns, launch missiles, and activate a camera. With his left hand on the throttle, he can key his radio, deploy speed brakes, elevate antennas, and make adjustments to other avionics with seven other buttons.

HOTAS is not without detractors. Some designers—and aviators, too—regard the proliferating "warts on a pickle" as self-defeating in their demands for dexterity. When someone suggested to an F-15 pilot that only a virtuoso pianist could play HOTAS, the aviator replied, "No, a virtuoso clarinetist."

A return to older technology is no solution. Instead, designers and engineers are working on ways that the aircraft can shoulder some of the pilot's work load—"watch his back" while his attention is directed toward the target out front. Taken together, the new technologies involved are expected to lead to the so-called supercockpit, intended for twenty-first-century fighters that are projected to follow the advanced tactical fighters that first flew in 1990.

Much of the pilot's burden is expected to be shifted to a computerized "intelligent autopilot," or "pilot's associate," that will serve as a combined copilot and backseater. Recognizing a pilot's voice, even when it is distorted by G forces and the tension of combat, the computer will be able to execute simple oral commands to change radio frequencies, report the amount of fuel on hand in a computer-synthesized voice of its own, control the radar, and select and fire a weapon.

The computerized associate can also be given the task of supplying information to the device intended to replace the head-up displays, which already display information needed to fly and fight. Though indispensable, a HUD has a serious shortcoming in combat, when a fighter pilot must constantly scan the skies for enemy planes: Only when he looks straight ahead can he see the information that the five-inch-square device offers.

Larger HUDs, measuring thirty inches by eighteen inches, could be a partial solution, but a full remedy lies in a concept that scientists term a "virtual cockpit"—a HUD in a helmet. The subject of earnest development in France and Japan, the headgear would be equipped with two miniature video projectors positioned to cast images onto the helmet's visor, which is always in the pilot's field of view no matter which way he looks. The visor will be transparent so the pilot can see through it to the world outside the cockpit. In addition, the pilot's associate could be programmed to analyze radar signals from defenses such as SAM sites and display a safe flight path between them. At night or in other conditions of poor visibility, the system could relay the plane's position, course, and speed to an on-board topographical database to generate an image of the terrain ahead.

It may be completely unnecessary for the pilot to glance inside the cockpit; he may well be able to call up images of instrument and control panels. As projected on his visor, they would appear to be at normal distance within the cockpit. Reaching out with his hand, the pilot could manipulate these computer-generated knobs and buttons as if they were real—even to the point of feeling the control and hearing a click in his earphones when a "button" is pressed. The means toward this end is the "touch simulator glove," which translates hand and finger movements into electronic signals that can be read by a computer and also simulates the pressure of fingertip against switch.

Engineers plan also for the pilot's associate to offer assistance in a fight by suggesting the appropriate offensive weapon or evasive tactic. In the case of a SAM launch, for example, the associate might advise dispensing chaff and flares. It could adjust a jammer to the frequency of a radar tracking the plane and recommend turning it on, and it could counsel a specific evasive maneuver, such as a diving break to right.

Should the plane go out of control, the computer would automatically recover for the pilot. (The Soviets have already built a less automated version of this feature into their Su-27 and MiG-29 fighters. On the instrument panel is a "panic button" that the pilot can press after he has departed the flight envelope. The plane reportedly will right itself from even the most vicious spin or tumble.) In the event of battle damage, the autopilot could be programmed to bias the controls and limit their movements so that the plane could be flown as usual, even though speed and maneuverability might be compromised. Set up to monitor an aviator's blood pressure, pulse rate, and breathing pattern, the system could take over the controls for an incapacitated flier, dive to a height of a few hundred feet

In a combat arena heavy with threats, a fighter pilot is hard-pressed to assimilate streams of data from his senses and his gauges. In the future, a computer will sort information into a graphic battle plan that is projected, in color and three dimensions, onto his helmet visor, as shown in the Air Force illustration at right.

These images will not block his view of the real world: Streetlights remain visible at lower left, as do ridges in the distance. And enemy planes will be visible as well.

To get a god's-eye view of the area, the pilot will consult the tactical situation display at lower right. The display shows his position on a grid *(vertical pink line)* along with the most immediate threats from SAM or antiaircraft batteries (red circles denote lethality envelopes). Below are aircraft-systems indicators and a weapons-status display. Missiles are prepared for firing by looking at the display and saying "Select and arm," then launched by a trigger on the stick.

For flying instructions, the pilot focuses on the large-scale projection. At left are airspeed (510 knots), compass heading (65 degrees), and an altitude bar (1,300 feet); his aircraft's attitude is represented by the white *W.* The sequence of pink open squares is the computer's recommended flight path; by following it, the pilot will skirt the antiaircraft artillery battery and end up on the tails of the two MiGs.

above the ground, for example, and fly to safety using the aircraft's terrain-avoidance radar.

Achieving this ambitious forecast will place monumental demands on computer programmers. Something on the order of 500,000 lines of programming will have to be woven into fail-safe software that can correctly respond to every conceivable combination of circumstances—as well as to any that may not be thought of in advance. Any such system will be very expensive, hardware and software together accounting for possibly one-third of the future fighter's flyaway cost. Yet through marvels of miniaturization, the entire avionics package, virtual cockpit and all, will amount only to about six percent of the aircraft's weight. With advances in helmet construction, for example, the new headgear would weigh slightly less than present helmets, and a topographical database for the entire world would contribute just four extra pounds.

Visionaries foresee a day when an aircraft filled with computers and their attendant sensors will obviate the need for an on-board pilot. They imagine missions being flown from the safety of reinforced bunkers or mobile command trailers by aviators seated behind video consoles or in cockpit simulators, their hands gripping stick and throttle to fight a distant battle as if it were a video game.

The advantages for aircraft design are obvious. Without the need for an oxygen system, an ejection seat, and other support systems

for a human, a fighter could carry more weapons and, limited only by the power of its engines and the strength of its materials, it could well perform maneuvers that would kill a pilot. But that is for a distant future. In the next generation, victory in aerial combat will still depend on a highly skilled aviator in the cockpit, and the job of technology will be to give him the edge over his opponent.

A Dogfight in the Future

The year was 2010, and the United States had just been called into armed confrontation with another nation. Two U.S. Air Force F-35 Bobcats were flying combat air patrol at 20,000 feet above the battle area. Their assignment was to provide top cover for a flight of A-22 fighter-bombers rolling in at low level to knock out an enemy tank column. Somewhere ahead the enemy's fighters would be climbing to the defense. Their mission was to blast through or evade the Bobcats and kill the A-22s.

For the pilot in the lead F-35—call sign Rodeo One-One—the targets first appeared on his three-dimensional holographic image of the battle area as four tiny fighters. Simultaneously, a calm female voice sounded in his ear. It was "Gertrude," his battle computer.

"Targets detected, confirmed hostile. Range three-eight-seven point six miles. Rate of closure two-two-four-six knots. Bearing constant at three-four-seven degrees. Display?"

"Display," ordered the flight leader. Gertrude instantly matched his voice pattern with her preprogrammed vocabulary, converting the sounds to digital signals for processing. In another split second, the targeting display illuminated, exposing four wedge-shaped "bandits" inside the lighted target-acquisition box.

"Confirm type," ordered the pilot.

"Scanning," said Gertrude. Then, "MiG-37. Threat parameters?"

"Negative." The pilot was thoroughly versed in the characteristics and armament of the '37. The Soviet-built aircraft was roughly comparable in performance to his own but exhibited certain weaknesses in electronics and air-to-air missilery. The flight leader knew that the oncoming MiGs could not have detected him yet, and that their missiles did not have quite the reach of his 150-mile, AIM-120B AMRAAMs. Since he was outnumbered two to one, the best tactic would be to engage as soon as the MiGs came within range—in about six minutes. He keyed his mike.

"Tallyho! Four bandits. You got 'em?" The message flashed to his wingman—Rodeo One-Two—in a microsecond burst on a direct beam that was immune to enemy interception.

"Roger, I'm going high, switching to IR," responded the wingman, indicating that he was shifting from radar to passive infrared tracking, which the enemy could not pick up.

"Roger One-Two. Cleared to fire after my run. Take what's left over." The flight leader's display showed his wingman rotating and going vertical. Fourteen seconds later, he rolled out at 40,000 feet, awaiting his turn to strike.

Rodeo One-One refocused his attention on the approaching MiG.

"Gertrude, acquire."

"Acquired," answered the battle computer.

"Stores," commanded the pilot.

His ordnance status brightened the upper right corner of his weapons-systems display, showing a top view of the weapons tucked into the missile bays inside the Bobcat's fuselage. Rodeo One-One selected his four AMRAAMs by pointing at them with his forefinger. A glove he wore transmitted the motion to Gertrude.

"Confirmed lock-on," Gertrude suddenly warned. Messages began to appear on the visor of the pilot's helmet, confirming that the F-35 had been located by the MiGs. In a matter of seconds he would be in range of the MiGs' AA-27 missiles, lethal affairs that could home not only on heat but also on a radar echo from his own aircraft. They could even be guided optically by the MiG-37 pilot. All he had to do was look at the target where it appeared in his own holographic display.

In the F-35, the readout "READY" glowed on Rodeo One-One's helmet visor, followed by the numerals 1, 2, 3, and 4 as each missile acknowledged its target programming.

"Action," the pilot commanded. The missile-bay doors opened, exposing the four deadly missiles on their launch rails. Simultaneously, the ejection seat rotated into a couchlike position to help his body endure the gut-wrenching turns of aerial combat, and his full-body G-suit tightened slightly as Gertrude partially inflated it in anticipation of what was to come. He could sustain up to fifteen Gs, but even if he blacked out, the computer would fly the plane until he regained consciousness.

"Target in range," announced the computer as the range finder digits projected onto the pilot's visor passed 158. Appearing to jump the gun by several miles, Gertrude was in fact compensating for pilot's and plane's reaction times.

"Fire!" The command had scarcely left the pilot's lips when he felt the slight jolt of four AIM-120Bs igniting and breaking away. As they streaked toward the onrushing MiGs, the pilot snapped the Bobcat around and began to climb just as the fates of the four AMRAAMs flashed on a screen: "MSL 1—HIT," followed by "MSL 2—HIT." He glanced at the screen for the next confirmation, but instead the notation "MSL 3—DES" blinked on. His third missile had been destroyed. Then "MISS," a word seldom seen after launching an AMRAAM, appeared next to "MSL 4."

Rodeo One-Two, meanwhile, had been monitoring the action from above. His own battle computer confirmed what he could see: The two surviving bandits, obviously jamming his radar, had vanished from the target display. But his infrared viewer picked them up, climbing straight toward him. They would be going for a shot.

His computer announced: "Launch detected. Two missiles. AA-27 radar guidance." At least one of the missiles was using its tracking radar, but the computer could say nothing about the second.

"Defend!" he ordered. Instantly five things happened: Flares shot from a pod in the Bobcat's tail, a cloud of metal confetti bloomed from the chaff dispenser, the F-35's ECM gear transmitted jamming signals in the AA-27's tracking band, the aircraft's System 23 activated and began painting a false radar target 300 meters to his right, and the Bobcat jinked violently left. The chaff, System 23, and ECM would likely defeat the AA-27's radar guidance system. If heat seeking had been selected by the MiG pilot for the other missile, the flares might decoy it. But if the missiles were being optically guided, it was up to the man in Rodeo One-Two.

"One missile closing," intoned the computer, confirming that only one of the AA-27s had been lured away.

Rodeo One-Two pulled into a tight climb, the canards straining under the load until he rolled out inverted and jerked back his nozzle lever. The vectored-thrust exhausts beneath the fuselage rotated, blasting him into a plummeting fallaway.

But it was too late. The AA-27, traveling at more than 4,000 knots, pulled almost fifty Gs as it followed the evading Bobcat and exploded less than forty feet below the left wing. Shrapnel tore into the fighter. Warning lights flashed red, actuated by 17 of some 600 sensors embedded in the "smart skin" of the aircraft. Luckily there was no fire, and one by one, the lights turned amber as the F-35's flight-control system began to compensate for the damage. The Bobcat could still fly.

As Rodeo One-Two was sorting out his situation, his leader rejoined the fray. Having climbed to 60,000 feet, Rodeo One-One now plunged downward at mach 2.5. Breaking through the bottom of a 45,000-foot cloud layer, he closed swiftly on the lead MiG. His quarry turned frantically. Then he vectored the thrust of his engines forward, slowing dramatically in an attempt to force the Bobcat into an overshoot. But vectoring his own thrust, Rodeo One-One turned inside the MiG and spoke two words: "Guns . . . FIRE!"

Instantly, Gertrude ran the speed-angle gunnery formula and shifted the nose of the aircraft twenty degrees ahead of the target, then triggered the cannon. Firing at 10,000 rounds per minute, it sounded less like a weapon than some monstrous air horn. The burst lasted less than two seconds. In that instant, 330 high-explosive 20-mm cannon projectiles left the muzzles of the gun's six spinning barrels—and the MiG burst into flame.

The Bobcat pilots scanned the sky. Gertrude advised that the lone surviving MiG was on full afterburner, racing for home. The fight was over. The future had arrived. ★

An F-15 Eagle flies a mission at dawn.

Acknowledgments

The editors of Time-Life Books wish to thank the following for their assistance in the preparation of this volume: Guy Aceto, *Air Force Magazine,* Arlington, Virginia; Captain Frank W. Ault (Ret.), Arlington, Virginia; Lieutenant Commander Dave Baranek, Pentagon, Washington, D.C.; Lieutenant Colonel Donald L. Black, Pentagon, Washington, D.C.; Lieutenant Colonel Bill Bledsoe, Pentagon, Washington, D.C.; Countess Maria Fede Caproni, Museo Aeronautico Di Taliedo, Rome; Kenneth Carter, Pentagon, Washington, D.C.; Federico Dalla Volta, Aeritalia, Rome; Vinh Ngoc Dang, Gaithersburg, Maryland; Colonel Charles DeBellevue, Misawa Air Base, Japan; Lorna Dodt, Pentagon, Washington, D.C.; Bill Dollard, Naval Air Station, Miramar, California; William Driscoll, Carlsbad, California; Lieutenant Colonel (Res.) David Eshel, Hod Hasharon, Israel; Patrick Facon, Service Historique de l'Armée de l'Air, Vincennes, France; Thomas Furness, University of Washington, Seattle, Washington; Don Haley, Ames-Dryden Flight Research Facility, Edwards, California; Commander Tom Hill, Hampton, Virginia; Hugh Howard, Pentagon, Washington, D.C.; Helen A. Kavanaugh, Wright-Patterson Air Force Base, Ohio; Ken Kilner, General Electric Simulation and Control Systems, Daytona Beach, Florida; General William Kirk, Alexandria, Virginia; James Kitchens, Maxwell Air Force Base, Montgomery, Alabama; Theo Klewitz, Fulda, Germany; Lieutenant Colonel Don Kline, Langley Air Force Base, Hampton, Virginia; Major Greg Kreis, Nellis Air Force Base, Nevada; John Labella, Hughes Aircraft Company, El Segundo, California; Franck Lazarus, Dassault Aviation, Vaucresson, France; Thomas Lindgren, Hughes/Raytheon, Canoga Park, California; Colonel (Res.) Oded Marom, Herzliya, Israel; Wayne Martin, Wright-Patterson Air Force Base, Ohio; Irene Miner, Pentagon, Washington, D.C.; Lyle Minter, Pentagon, Washington, D.C.; Ishigaki Misao, Nihon Denpa News, Tokyo; David Moorehouse, Wright-Patterson Air Force Base, Ohio; Blake Morrison, *Fighter Weapons Review,* Las Vegas, Nevada; Ed Murphy, Medal of Honor Historical Society, Mesa, Arizona; Meinrad Nilges, Bundesarchiv, Koblenz, Germany; Michael E. O'Grady, Vienna, Virginia; Nicholas Oresko, Congressional Medal of Honor Society, New York, New York; Lieutenant Tom Page, Navy Fighter Weapons School, San Diego, California; Gianni Pasqua, Aeritalia, Rome; General (Res.) Benjamin Peled, Jerusalem; Debbie Reed, Pentagon, Washington, D.C.; Gerry Reeves, Jerry Ringer, Cubic Corporation, San Diego, California; Major Scotty Rogers, Pentagon, Washington, D.C.; Lieutenant Colonel Robert Schraeder, Pentagon, Washington, D.C.; Bettie Sprigg, Pentagon, Washington, D.C.; George Stimson, San Marino, California; Captain Susan Strednansky, Pentagon, Washington, D.C.; T. R. Swartz, Cubic Defense Systems, San Diego, California; C. G. Sweeting, Clinton, Maryland; Bill Sweetman, Oakdale, Minnesota; Mabel Thomas, Pentagon, Washington, D.C.; Warren Thompson, Germantown, Tennessee; Senator Leo K. Thorsness, Seattle, Washington; Major Anthony William Valentino, Navy Fighter Weapons School, San Diego, California; Major Del Weber (Ret.), Yuma, Arizona; Bob Wendt, San Diego, California; Colonel Karl Whittenberg, Pentagon, Washington, D.C.; Robin Whittle, Air Force Association, Arlington, Virginia; Lieutenant David J. Wray, Pentagon, Washington, D.C.

Bibliography

BOOKS

Armitage, Sir Michael, *Unmanned Aircraft.* London: Brassey's, 1988.

Bonds, Ray, editor, *The Vietnam War: The Illustrated History of the Conflict in Southeast Asia.* New York: Crown Publishers, 1979.

Brown, Ashley, *War in Peace.* New York: Marshall Cavendish, 1985.

Brown, Neville, *The Future of Air Power.* New York: Holmes & Meier Publishers, 1986.

Campbell, Christopher, *Air Warfare: The Fourth Generation.* New York: Arco Publishing, 1984.

Cunningham, Randy, and Jeff Ethell, *Fox Two: The Story of America's First Ace in Vietnam.* New York: Warner Books, 1984.

Dorr, Robert F.:
Air War Hanoi. London: Blandford Press, 1988.
Vietnam MiG Killers: Deadly Duel over Vietnam. Osceola, Wisconsin: Motorbooks International, 1988.

Drendel, Lou, *USAF Phantoms in Combat.* Carrollton, Texas: Squadron/Signal Publications, 1987.

Dutton, Lyn, *Military Space.* London: Brassey's, 1990.

Eschmann, Karl J., *The Untold Story of the Air Raids over North Vietnam.* New York: Ivy Books, 1989.

Ethell, Jeffrey, and Alfred Price, *One Day in a Long War: May 10, 1972, Air War, North Vietnam.* New York: Random House, 1989.

Francillon, René J., *Vietnam: The War in the Air.* New York: Arch Cape Press, 1987.

Futrell, R. Frank, et al., *Aces & Aerial Victories: The United States Air Force in Southeast Asia 1965-1973.* Maxwell Air Force Base, Alabama: Office of Air Force History, Headquarters, USAF, 1976.

Gunston, Bill:
An Illustrated Guide to Future Fighters and Combat Aircraft. New York: Prentice Hall Press, 1984.
An Illustrated Guide to Modern Airborne Missiles. New York: Prentice Hall Press, 1986.

Gunston, Bill, and Mike Spick, *Modern Air Combat.* New York: Crown Publishers, 1983.

Hall, George, *Top Gun: The Navy's Fighter Weapons School.* Novato, California: Presidio Press, 1987.

Jane's All the World's Aircraft 1987-88. New York: Jane's Publishing, 1987.

Jane's All the World's Aircraft 1990-91. Edited by

Mark Lambert. Alexandria, Virginia: Jane's Information Group, 1990.

Jane's Weapon Systems 1983-84. Edited by Ronald T. Pretty. New York: Jane's Publishing, 1983.

Johnson, Air Vice Marshal J. E. "Johnnie," *The Story of Air Fighting.* London: Hutchinson, 1985.

Mason, Air Vice Marshal R. A., *Air Power: An Overview of Roles.* London: Brassey's, 1987.

Mason, Air Vice Marshal R.A., editor, *War in the Third Dimension: Essays in Contemporary Air Power.* New York: Brassey's Defence Publishers.

Middleton, Drew, *Air War Vietnam.* New York: Arno Press, 1978.

The Military Frontier, by the Editors of Time-Life Books (Understanding Computers series). Alexandria, Virginia: Time-Life Books, 1988.

Miller, Jay, *The X-Planes.* Arlington, Texas: Aerofax, 1988.

Morrocco, John, and the Editors of Boston Publishing Company:
Rain of Fire: Air War, 1969-1973 (The Vietnam Experience series). Boston: Boston Publishing Company, 1985.
Thunder from Above: Air War, 1941-1968 (The Vietnam Experience series). Boston: Boston Publishing Company, 1984.

O'Ballance, Edgar, *No Victor, No Vanquished: The Yom Kippur War.* San Rafael, California: Presidio Press, 1978.

Parsons, Iain, editor, *The Encyclopaedia of Air Warfare.* New York: Thomas Y. Crowell Company, 1975.

Richardson, Doug, *Stealth.* New York: Orion Books, 1989.

Scutts, Jerry, *Wolf-Pack: Hunting MiGs over Vietnam.* New York: Warner Books, 1988.

Shaw, Robert L., *Fighter Combat: Tactics and Maneuvering.* Annapolis, Maryland: Naval Institute Press, 1985.

Siuru, Bill, and John D. Busick, *Future Flight: The Next Generation of Aircraft Technology.* Blue Ridge Summit, Pennsylvania: Tab Books, 1987.

Skinner, Michael, *Air Combat for the '80s: Red Flag.* Novato, California: Presidio Press, 1984.

Spick, Mike, *The Ace Factor: Air Combat and the Role of Situational Awareness.* Annapolis, Maryland: Naval Institute Press, 1988.

Sweetman, Bill:
Advanced Fighter Technology. Osceola, Wisconsin: Motorbooks International, 1987.
Aircraft 2000: The Future of Aerospace Technology. New York: Crown Publishers, 1984.
The Presidio Concise Guide to Soviet Military Aircraft. Novato, California: Presidio Press, 1981.

Taylor, Michael J. H., *Jet Warplanes: The Twenty-First Century.* New York: Exeter Books, 1986.

Ulanoff, Brigadier General Stanley M., and Lieutenant Colonel David Eshel, *The Fighting Israeli Air Force.* New York: Arco Publishing, 1985.

Walker, Bryce, and the Editors of Time-Life Books, *Fighting Jets* (The Epic of Flight series). Alexandria, Virginia: Time-Life Books, 1983.

Walker, Air Vice Marshal John R., *Air Superiority Operations.* New York: Brassey's, 1989.

The World's Great Interceptor Aircraft. New York: W. H. Smith, 1989.

PERIODICALS

"AAAM," *International Defense Review,* August 1990.

Blesse, Major General, "No Guts No Glory," *USAF Fighter Weapons Review,* spring 1973.

Cary, Peter, "The Pentagon's Misguided Missile: How Efforts to Build the AMRAAM Wrought Conflicts and High Costs," *U.S. News & World Report,* May 1, 1989.

"Chemical Reaction," *Time,* January 16, 1989.

Cignatta, John V., "A U.S. Pilot Looks at the Order of Battle, Bekáa Valley Operations," *Military Electronics/Countermeasures,* February 1983.

Coram, Robert, "Military Shooting Galleries: War Games on a Video Screen," *Atlanta Constitution,* August 1, 1982.

Cutter, Paul S., editor, "ELTA Plays a Decisive Role in the EOB Scenario," *Military Electronics/Countermeasures,* January 1983.

Dornheim, Michael A., "ATF Prototypes Outstrip F-15 in Size and Thrust," *Aviation Week & Space Technology,* September 17, 1990.

Dudney, Robert S., "The ATF and Its Friends," *Air Force Magazine,* January 1989.

"Eagle vs. MiG," *Born in Battle Magazine,* No. 13, 1980.

"Electronic Air Combat Training," *Asian Defence Journal* (Malaysia), May 1983.

Elgcrona, Per-Olov, "The Electrical Flight Control System (EFCS) of the Gripen Is a Full Authority, Fly-By-Wire System with No Mechanical Back-Up," *The Saab-Scania Griffin,* October 1989.

"Ericsson Displays, Signal Processing Aid Pilots of Multimission Aircraft," *Aviation Week & Space Technology,* July 2, 1990.

EuroFighter Review, September 1990.

"F/A-18 360 Combat Simulator," *National Defense Magazine,* November 1985.

Flamm, Don, "Combat Realism with Cubic Air Combat Training Systems," *Asian Defence Journal* (Malaysia), August 1989.

Geisenheyner, Stefan, "Computer-Generated Imagery in Flight Training," *Armada International,* October/November 1988.

Golding, George, "Combat Aces of the 1980s in Instant Replay," *San Mateo Times,* April 25, 1981.

" 'Good Kill! Good Kill!' " *Newsweek,* January 16, 1989.

Henderson, Captain David W. (Ret.), and Minton B. Cronkhite, "Train Where You Fight," *U.S. Naval Institute Proceedings,* (Annapolis, Maryland), December 1986.

Hewish, Mark, Anthony Robinson, and Gérard Turbé, "Air-to-Air Missiles," *International Defense Review,* August 1990.

"The IAF Eagle Squadrons," *Military Enthusiast,* Vol. 6, No. 33.

Kandebo, Stanley W., "Modified F-15B to Demonstrate STOL, Maneuver Capability," *Aviation Week & Space Technology,* May 29, 1989.

Kinnucan, Paul, "Superfighters: New Generation of Agile, Stealthy Supersonic Fighters Should Assure Air Superiority for the 1990s," *High Technology,* April 1984.

Magnuson, Ed, "Chemical Reaction," *Time,* January 16, 1989.

Mancus, Peter, "Top Gun: The Deadly Art of Air

Combat Maneuvering as Taught at the Navy's Toughest Graduate School," *Airpower*, May 1982.

Mascot, Captain Thomas K., and Captain Mark G. Beasley, "The Bandit's Alive at the Merge," *USAF Fighter Weapons Review*, winter 1985.

Mayo, Major Charles E., "Lebanon: An Air Defense Analysis," *Air Defense Artillery*, winter 1983.

Modin, Karl-Erik, "The Choice of the Unstable Delta-Canard Configuration for the JAS 39 Gripen Was Based on Multi-Role Requirements for Fighter Aircraft," *The Saab-Scania Griffin*, October 1989.

Mol, Colonel William D., "Rules of Engagement," *USAF Fighter Weapons Review*, spring 1973.

O'Connor, Michael, "Aces of the Yellow Star," *Air Aces of the Vietnam War*, summer 1987.

Parsons, Lieutenant Commander Dave, "Top Gun at Twenty!" *Airpower*, January 1989.

"Photos Show Key Features of YF-23A ATF," *Aviation Week & Space Technology*, July 9, 1990.

Porteous, Holly, "Adapting to New Needs," *Jane's Defence Weekly*, June 30, 1990.

Ravenstein, Charles A., "Operation Bolo," *Air War over Vietnam*, winter 1984.

Reed, Fred, "The Electric Jet," *Air & Space*, December 1986/January 1987.

Rhea, John, "The Simulator Revolution," *Air Force Magazine*, December 1989.

Rhodes, Jeffrey P., "The Fast-Moving World of Simulation," *Air Force Magazine*, December 1988.

Saw, David, "The Uses of Flight Simulation," *NATO's Sixteen Nations*, June 1989.

Schwartzbrod, Alexandra, "Rafale Basks in Its Security, if Not in Farnborough Spotlight," *Armed Forces Journal International*, September 1990.

Scott, William B., "YF-23A Previews Design Features of Future Fighters," *Aviation Week & Space Technology*, July 2, 1990.

Snir, Asher, "A Pilot's Requiem." Translated by Arye Ephrath. *Air & Space*, October/November 1988.

Streetley, Martin, "Eagles in the Sky: Israeli Air Force—Lebanon 1982," *The Elite*, Vol. 2, Issue 23.

"Stretching the Capability Quotient," *Vectors Magazine*, No. 2, 1986.

Sweetman, Bill, "YF-23 Rolls Out in California," *Jane's Defence Weekly*, June 30, 1990.

Thompson, Steven L., "A New Era for Man and Machine," *Washington Post*, May 10, 1987.

Thompson, Warren, "Wolves in Wolves Clothing,' *Airpower*, March 1990.

Timmerman, Kenneth R., "France Going Solo with Rafale," *Defense Electronics*, June 1987.

Varni, Gerard, " 'MiGs' over Nevada—Red Flag," *International Combat Arms*, May 1989.

Weger, Peter, "EFA Development Status Report," *Military Technology*, September 1990.

"Why Basic Flight Training Facilities Can't Be Consolidated," *Government Executive*, August 1983.

Wilshere, Kevin B., "Fighters for the '90s," *Military Technology*, June 1987.

"YF-23 Shows Stealth Features," *Jane's Defence Weekly*, July 7, 1990.

OTHER SOURCES

Ames Research Center, "X-29 Shows Unexpected Maneuverability in 'High-Alpha' Flight." Pamphlet. Edwards, California: Ames Research Center, April 9, 1990.

"F-15 Short Takeoff and Landing/Maneuver Technology Demonstrator (S/MTD)." PAM No. 90-102. Wright-Patterson Air Force Base, Ohio, July 1990.

"F-22 Lockheed-Boeing General Dynamics." Brochure. Burbank, California: Lockheed Corporation, September 1990.

Hills, George, "System Description." Manual. Hughes Aircraft Company, Herndon, Virginia.

"JAS 39 Gripen: The Combat Aircraft for the 21st Century." Brochure. Linkoping, Sweden: Saab-Scania.

Lambeth, Benjamin S., *Moscow's Lessons from the 1982 Lebanon Air War (June 1982)*. Santa Monica, California: The Rand Publications Series, September 1984.

Nordeen, Lon, "Fighters over Israel: The Story of the Israeli Air Force from the War of Independence to the Bekáa Valley." Unpublished manuscript. Orion Books, New York.

"Rafale." Brochure. Dassault Aviation, Vaucresson, France.

Stimpson, George W., "Introduction to Airborne Radar." Brochure. El Segundo, California: Hughes Aircraft Company, 1983.

Stucky, Captain Paul R., "F-15 Basic Fighter Maneuvers, Course F1500IDOPN, F-15." Instructional Text. Nellis Air Force Base, Nevada, October 1982.

"TACTS/ACMI/MDS: The World's Finest Air Combat Training Systems." Cubic Defense Systems, 1989.

Vietnamese Stamps, provided by Dr. James Kitchens, Maxwell Air Force Base, Alabama.

"YF-23 Advanced Tactical Fighter Prototype a Revolution in Air Superiority." Brochure. Hawthorne, California: Northrop McDonnell Douglas, August 1990.

Index

materials, 147-148, 155; remotely piloted, 160, 162; size, 152; speed, 148, 149; stealth technology, 153, *154*, 155-156; steering, 149-150; wings, *140*, *146-147. See also* Eurofighter; Gripen; Rafale; YF-22; YF-23
Fighting Falcon. *See* F-16
Flanker. *See* Su-27
Flares: *66-67*, 153
Flight envelope: 129-130
Flogger. *See* MiG-23
Fly-by-light (FBL) controls: 150
Fly-by-wire (FBW) controls: 130, 143, 149
Frequency modulation ranging: *100*
Fulcrum. *See* MiG-29

G

Galland, Adolf: 132
GCI. *See* Ground control intercept
General Dynamics: 87, 145
G-forces: 156-157
Gripen. *See* JAS-39
Ground clutter: *101, 103*
Ground control intercept (GCI) tactics: 29
Grumman: 90
G-suit: 156-157
Gun, Gatling: 28, 150
Guns: on modern fighters, 22-23
Gypsy (call sign): 17

H

Harrier: 141, *149; vs.* F-14, 142-144
Hawkeye. *See* E-2C
Head-up display (HUD): 20, 85, 158; future, 158-159, *160-161*
Hed, Operation: 70, 71
Helmets: 29
High yo-yo: *58-59*, 60, 61, 62, 64, 66
Homestead Air Force Base: 134
HOTAS (hands-on throttle and stick): 157
HUD. *See* Head-up display
Hughes: 85

I

IAF. *See* Israel: Air Force
Infrared homing: *46*
Institute of Strategic Studies (London): 71
Intelligent autopilot. *See* Pilot's associate
Iraq: nuclear reactor attacked, 87; U.S. confrontation with, 97
Israel: 69, *map* 72; air combat with Egypt, *68*, *78-79*, *80-81*, 82; air combat in Lebanon, 69-70, 82, *86*, 87, *88-89*, 90-91, *92-93*, 94-95; air combat with Soviet forces, 71-74; air combat with Syria, 74-77, 80, 82, 83, 87, *88-89*, 90-91, *92-93*, 94-95; Air Force (IAF), 69, 70, 71, 73, 78, 80, *86*, 87; attack on Beirut, *96-97*; attack on Iraqi nuclear

reactor, 87; noise raid on Cairo, 70; remotely piloted vehicles, 90; training of pilots, *78-79*, 112; War of Attrition, 74, 94; Yom Kippur War, 77, *78-79*, *80-81*, 82

J

Jaguar: 112
JAS-39 (Gripen): *142-143*, 145
John F. Kennedy, USS: 17; Squadron VF-32, 17-21
Johnson, Harold: 43
Johnson, Lyndon B.: 44

K

Katyusha rockets: 87
KC-135: 43
Kfir C2: 86, 92, 112, 147
Kirk, William: 36

L

Lag pursuit: *56-57*
Lebanon: 70; air combat in, 69-70, 82, *86*, 87, *88-89*, 90-91, *92-93*, 94-95; Beirut, *96-97*; Bekáa Valley, 87
Libya: U.S. air combat with, 17, *18-19*, 20-21
Lockheed: 145
Low yo-yo: *56-57*, 64
Lufbery Circle: 51

M

M-61: 150
McDonnell Douglas: 83, 141, 145
Mastiff: 90
Materials: 147-148, 155
Maverick. *See* AGM-65
Medal of Honor, Congressional: 43
MFD. *See* Multifunction display
MiG-15: in Southeast Asia, 27
MiG-17: 78; armament, 30; Egyptian, *78-79*; in Southeast Asia, 25, 27, *29*, 30, 32, 43, *50-51*; Syrian, 74-77
MiG-21: 78; armament, 31; Egyptian, *68*, 71, 82; in Southeast Asia, 30, *31*, 32, 41-42, 43, 49; Syrian, 83, 87, *88-89*, 93, 94
MiG-21 (Fishbed J): 71, 110, 124-125; in Middle East, 71, 72, 73
MiG-23 (Flogger): 83, 110, 125; Libyan, *18-19*, 20-21; Syrian, 83, 87, 93, 94
MiG-25 (Foxbat): 83
MiG-29 (Fulcrum): 84, 110, 125, 159; dogfight tactics, *54-55*, *56-57*, *58-59*, *60-61*, *62-63*, *64-65*, *66-67*; upgrading, 146
MiGCAP: 30
Mirage: 145
Mirage IIIC: Israeli, *68*, 73, 75
Mirage 2000: 112; computer control, 130; upgrading, 146
Miramar Naval Air Station: 45, 128
Missiles, air-to-air: *46-47*; electro-

magnetic homing, *46-47*; infrared, *46*; new generation, 151, *152-153*; reliability, 23, 35-36, 53, 94-95. *See also* Alkali; Atoll; Phoenix; Sidewinder; Sparrow
Missiles, air-to-ground: 91. *See also* AGM-
Missiles, surface-to-air (SAM): 40, 71, 80; in Bekáa Valley, 87, 90-91, 92, 95; spacing of sites, 156. *See also* SA-
Multifunction display (MFD): 157

N

N (captain): 79
Nasser, Gamal Abdul: 70, 74
Nellis Air Force Base: 45, 111-113, 118
Nguyen Van Bay: *29*, 33
Nimitz, USS: *10-11*
Nixon, Richard M.: 45
Northrop: 141, 145
North Vietnamese Air Force (NVAF): forces and tactics, 27, 28-30, 32-33; stamps commemorating, *32*

O

OH-58 (Kiowa): 112
Olds, Robin: 38, *39*, 40-42, 43

P

Palestine Liberation Organization (PLO): 87
Panavia: 146
Peace for Galilee, Operation: 87
Phantom. *See* F-4
Phoenix: 131, 151, 152
Pilot's associate: 158-159, *160-161*
Pratt & Whitney: 84
Pulse-delay ranging: *98-99*
Pulse-repetition frequency (PRF): *98-103*, *104-105*
Python III: 93, 95

Q

Qadhafi, Muammar al-: 17

R

Radar: 98; AEW, 90; cockpit display, *104-105*; frequency modulation ranging, *100*; ground clutter, *101, 103*; look-down, 90, *101*; in missile proximity fuse, 151; pulse-delay ranging, *98-99*; pulse-Doppler, 85, 98, *101-105*; pulse-repetition frequency, *98-105. See also* Stealth technology
Radar cross section (RCS): *154*, 155
Radar intercept officer (RIO): 19, 34, *106*, 131, *134*, 135-139
Rafale: *142-143*, 145
Raines, Ella: 39
Ramjet: 151, *152-153*
Range training officer (RTO): 115

Picture Credits

The sources for the illustrations that appear in this book are listed below. Credits from left to right are separated by semicolons, from top to bottom by dashes.
Cover: Mark Meyer. 2, 3: McDonnell Douglas Corp. 4, 5: Cliff Feulner/Image Bank. 6, 7: George Hall/Check Six. 8-11: Co Rentmeester. 16: U.S. Navy Photo No. DN-SC-87-04758. 18, 19: U.S. Navy(4)—art by Time-Life Books, Inc.(4). 22, 23: Dennis Brack/DoD Pool. 24: Larry Burrows for LIFE. 26, 27: Jack Swaney, Donald L. Heilinger Collection. 29: Camera Press, London. 31: UPI/Bettmann. 32: Laurence Cantrell, courtesy James H. Kitchens III, Auburn, Alabama. 34, 35: Hugh R. Muir. 39: U.S. Air Force Photo No. SDAN/102291. 40, 41: Art by Fred Holz. 43: Doug Wilson, courtesy Senator Leo K. Thorsness; courtesy Senator Leo K. Thorsness. 46, 47:

Art by Matt McMullen. 50: U.S. Navy Photo No. SDAN 1151716. 52: U.S. Air Force, courtesy Colonel Steve Ritchie. 54-67: Art by Paul Salmon. 68: From *Israel Air Force*, edited by Oded Marom, published by the Ministry of Defense/Air Force Command. 72: Mapping Specialists Ltd. 78, 79: AP/Wide World Photos. 80, 81: Government Press Office Photo, courtesy Eshel-Dramit, Jerusalem. 84, 85: From *Military Aircraft of the World*, by Hiroshi Seo, published by Jane's Publishing Co., Ltd., 1981. 86: David Eshel, Jerusalem. 88, 89: From *Israel Air Force*, edited by Oded Marom, published by the Ministry of Defense/Air Force Command. 92, 93: AP/Wide World Photos. 96, 97: Neveu/Gamma-Liaison. 98-103: Art by Stephen R. Wagner. 104, 105: U.S. Air Force Photo by T. Sgt. Fernando Serna/*Airman* magazine, art by Time-Life Books, Inc. 106: George Hall/Check Six. 108, 109: U.S. Air Force Photo by Major Gregory Kreis. 110: Bundesarchiv, Koblenz. 114, 115: Art by John Snyder, photos Cubic Corporation. 118, 119: Warren E. Thompson. 120, 121: Training and Support Systems Group of Hughes Aircraft Company; art by Steve Bauer. 122, 123: Art by Steve Bauer. 126-129: Robert W. Wendt. 132-133: David Hathcox/Arms Communications. 134-139: Larry Sherer, Homestead Air Force Base, Florida/Cubic Corporation. 140: Northrop Corp. Photo. 142: Alain Ernoult, Paris. 143: B. Wall/Saab-Scania AB—Aeritalia, Rome. 144, 145: Lockheed Aeronautical Systems Company, photo by YF-22 Photographic Team. 146, 147: Art by Mark Robinson. 148, 149: U.S. Air Force. 152, 153: Art by Fred Holz. 154: McDonnell Douglas, St. Louis, Missouri—Northrop Corp. Photo. 160, 161: Art by Kim Barnes of Stansbury, Ronsaville, Wood Inc. 166, 167: Co Rentmeester.

TIME ® LIFE BOOKS

Time-Life Books is a division of Time Life Inc., a wholly owned subsidiary of
THE TIME INC. BOOK COMPANY

TIME-LIFE BOOKS

MANAGING EDITOR: Thomas H. Flaherty
Director of Editorial Resources: Elise D. Ritter-Clough
Director of Photography and Research:
John Conrad Weiser
Editorial Board: Dale M. Brown, Roberta Conlan, Laura Foreman, Lee Hassig, Jim Hicks, Blaine Marshall, Rita Thievon Mullin, Henry Woodhead

PUBLISHER: Joseph J. Ward

Associate Publisher: Anne Mirabito
Editorial Director: Russell B. Adams, Jr.
Marketing Director: Anne Everhart
Director of Design: Louis Klein
Production Manager: Prudence G. Harris
Supervisor of Quality Control: James King

Editorial Operations
Production: Celia Beattie
Library: Louise D. Forstall
Computer Composition: Deborah G. Tait (Manager), Monika D. Thayer, Janet Barnes Syring, Lillian Daniels

Correspondents: Elisabeth Kraemer-Singh (Bonn); Christine Hinze (London); Christina Lieberman (New York); Maria Vincenza Aloisi (Paris); Ann Natanson (Rome). Valuable assistance was also provided by Elizabeth Brown, Katheryn White (New York), Mieko Ikeda (Tokyo), Marlin Levin (Jerusalem), Ann Wise (Rome).

THE NEW FACE OF WAR

SERIES EDITOR: Lee Hassig
Series Administrator: Judith W. Shanks
Art Director: Christopher M. Register

Editorial Staff for *Air Combat*
Picture Editor: Charlotte Marine Fullerton
Associate Editors/Research: Robin Currie, Susan M. Klemens, Gwen C. Mullen
Assistant Editors/Research: Jennifer L. Pearce, Mark Rogers
Assistant Art Director: Fatima Taylor
Writers: Charles J. Hagner, James M. Lynch
Copy Coordinators: Elizabeth Graham (principal), Anthony K. Pordes
Editorial Assistant: Kathleen S. Walton
Picture Coordinator: Barry Anthony

Special Contributors: Clifford Beal, Anthony Chiu, Champ Clark, George Constable, Rita Dallas, George Daniels, Jon Guttman, Thomas Horne, Jerry Korn, John Lang, Brian Pohanka, Craig Roberts, Charles Smith, Diane Ullius (text); Douglas Brown, Katya Sharpe Cooke, John Davidson, Ellen Gross, John Hackett, Rod Lenahan, John Raskauskas, Jacqueline Shaffer, Barbara Jones Smith, Christian Smith, Christine Soares, Ron Wagner (research); Sue Ellen Pratt, Tyrone Taylor (art); Mel Ingber (index).

Library of Congress Cataloging in Publication Data
Air combat/by the editors of Time-Life Books.
    p. cm.   (The New face of war series).
    Includes bibliographical references and index.
    ISBN 0-8094-8604-0
    1. Fighter plane combat.
I. Time-Life Books. II. Series.
UG700.A56 1991
358.4'3—dc20   90-20800 CIP
ISBN 0-8094-8605-9 (lib. bdg.)

Time-Life Books Inc. offers a wide range of fine recordings including a *Rock 'n' Roll Era* series. For subscription information, call 1-800-621-7026 or write Time-Life Music, P.O. Box C-32068, Richmond, Virginia 23261-2068.